"Having a conversation with my father, it was a mind-opening experience. He viewed the world differently. If you'd just be driving down the road and he looked out the window, and you looked out the window, he saw something different. . . .

Everything he did, and everywhere he looked, he was looking for ideas about sculpture and art. He lived, breathed, and thought about making artwork, all the time."

—WINIFRED FORRESTER

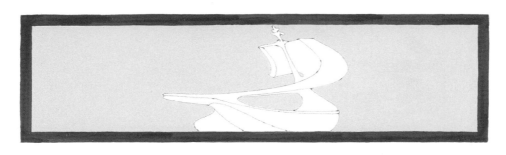

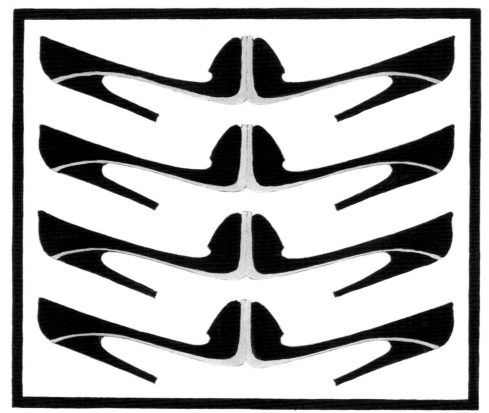

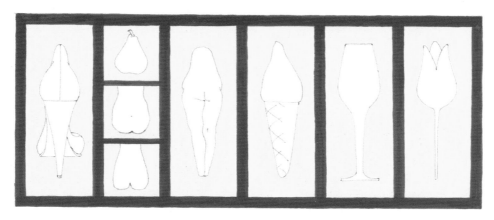

Shoe Fantasies Series: 479   The Shoe as Related Form I   Forrester

A MIND IN MOTION: THE ART OF
CHARLES H. FORRESTER

CURATED BY
WINIFRED FORRESTER

A MIND IN MOTION: THE ART OF CHARLES H. FORRESTER
COPYRIGHT © 2020, FOLLY INDUSTRIES, LLC

FIRST EDITION: 2020
PRINTED IN THE UNITED STATES OF AMERICA.

ISBN: 978-0-578-67826-9 (HARDCOVER)
ISBN: 978-0-578-67827-6 (EBOOK)

Publisher's Cataloging-in-Publication Data

Forrester, Winifred, 1958–
A Mind In Motion : The Art Of Charles H. Forrester / curated by Winifred Forrester.
Nashville, TN: Folly Industries, LLC, 2020. | Includes bibliographical references.
ISBN: 978-0-578-67826-9 (hardcover) | 978-0-578-67827-6 (ebook)
LCSH Forrester, Charles H. | Sculptors—United States—20th century. |
   Sculpture, American—
20th century—Pictorial works. | BISAC ART / Sculpture & Installation |
   BIOGRAPHY & AUTOBIOGRAPHY / Artists, Architects, Photographers
Classification: LCC NB212 .F67 2020 | DDC 730/.973—dc23

COVER: Fig. 523 *Figure Head,* 1983
FRONTIS: Fig. 479.5 *Shoe as Related Form I,* 1979
PAGE 9: Forrester assembling *The Blue Sphere,* Fig. 434

BOOK AND COVER DESIGN BY
MARY SUSAN OLESON, BLU DESIGN CONCEPTS

FOLLY INDUSTRIES, LLC
P.O. BOX 280663
NASHVILLE, TN 37228

THE DOCUMENTARY

A Line Unbroken: The Charles Forrester Story

A FOLLY INDUSTRIES, LLC MEDIA PRODUCTION

AN EXCEPTIONALLY GIFTED sculptor and artist, Charles H. Forrester (1928-2010) left his unique imprint on this world—his artwork spans six decades and captures a multitude of mediums and styles.

The documentary, *A Line Unbroken: The Charles Forrester Story,* honors his legacy and noteworthy contributions to the art world. The film will preview in the summer of 2020 in conjunction with an exhibit featuring the late sculptor's work at the Downing Museum in Bowling Green, Kentucky. In addition, the documentary will be submitted for consideration in various film festivals.

A professor at Western Kentucky University in Bowling Green for almost thirty years, Forrester and his work directly impacted generations of sculptors and artists.

Commissioned by the Forrester family, the film was produced by David and Patricia Earnhardt of Earnhardt Films, LLC of Nashville, Tennessee.

More information about the documentary and art exhibit
is available at: www.charlesforrester.com.

TABLE OF CONTENTS

THE BOOK IS DEDICATED to the memory of our mother, Dorothy Reese Forrester (1924-2004), and all the women from that era who took a back seat in order to fully embrace their husbands' spotlight, all the while playing an essential supporting role to ensure their success.

Our mother was a gifted writer, intellectual, linguist, and political commentator extraordinaire in the family home. She dearly loved her family and most of all, our father. She ghost-wrote his artist statements, edited his thesis, typed, acted as publicist and agent, and was his muse for most of her life. She is to be celebrated as the essential half of a partnership that spanned fifty-three years.

"AS A SCULPTOR I endeavor to interpret some aspect of the spiritual reality. I feel orientated toward a spiritual reality rather than nature because I regard nature as merely a reflection of the spiritual reality. I believe that it is not enough that a sculptor's work mirror the confusion of his times. It is the artist's duty to seek meaning in chaos."

—CHARLES FORRESTER, 1960

ACKNOWLEDGEMENTS by Winifred Forrester

This book, *A MIND IN MOTION: The Art of Charles H. Forrester,* and the short documentary, *A Line Unbroken: The Charles Forrester Story,* are powerful examples of how many people came together to honor my father's work because they believed it worthy to be recognized and remembered for generations to come.

I met many new people and rekindled old friendships during the process of curating the collection of my father's artwork and working to bring his life's passion to a larger audience. I came to fully appreciate life's lesson that one is only as successful as the relationships cultivated during one's life. I am indebted to the amazingly creative people that made this project happen, and I want to acknowledge them all.

DR. GUY JORDAN, Associate Professor of Art History, Western Kentucky University (WKU), for his keen insight and the introduction to this book.

RUSS FAXON, sculptor extraordinaire and my dad's former student, for his contributions to the book and film and always being there when I called for help.

SAM HUNT, Adjunct Professor of Art, WKU, for his enthusiasm and poignant memories of my father and his artwork.

To all the people, present and past, at WKU who gave their time, energy, and talent to make this project happen:

KRISTINA ARNOLD, Professor and Art Department Head
PRESIDENT TIM CABONI
BARBARA DEEB, WKYU-FM Public Radio
DONNIE FIRKINS, former student and stone sculptor
JEFF JENSEN, Associate Professor, Graphic Design
DAVID LEE, University Historian

JACK LESIEUR, Director, Downing Museum
DAVID MARQUEZ, Assistant Professor of Sculpture
NEIL PETERIE, former colleague and professor
SANDRA STAEBELL, Curator, Kentucky Museum

CAROLINE PHILLIPS at the Jordan Schnitzer Museum of Art, who provided a compelling West Coast interpretation of *The Equestrian* statue.

JOE NOLAN, for his crisp, relevant descriptions of the categories and series of artwork included in the book.

TONY NOVAK, for his encouragement and careful, painstaking conservation, and for his restoration work on the sculptures.

To the best professional team from Dexterity Books: MATT WEST, CEO, ELIZABETH MAYNARD GARRETT, editor, and MARY SUSAN OLESON, designer.

DEVI SANFORD, photographer, for bringing to life all the sculpture in the Forrester Family Art Collection.

DAVID AND PATRICIA EARNHARDT of Earnhardt Films, LLC for their amazing film production skills.

GREG WASSOM, Vice-President, and SHALA HUDSON, Executive Assistant, U.S. Bank, a major supporter of the Arts in Bowling Green, Kentucky.

TO MY BROTHER, JOHN, AND HIS WIFE, ELISABETH, who provided insight and encouragement from their home in Italy.

AT LAST BUT NOT LEAST, MY CHILDREN, ISABELLA AND MERONICA, AND THEIR FATHER, BOBBY KENT, for enduring countless hours without me while I worked on this project.

ABOUT THE CONTRIBUTORS

DR. GUY JORDAN
Associate Professor of Art History
Western Kentucky University

JOHN FORRESTER
Son of Charles H. Forrester
Rome, Italy

WINIFRED FORRESTER
Daughter of Charles H. Forrester
Nashville, Tennessee

RUSS FAXON
Former student and figurative bronze sculptor
Bell Buckle, Tennessee

JOE NOLAN
Multi-talented musician, writer, and intermedia artist
Nashville, Tennessee

CAROLINE PHILLIPS
Jordan Schnitzer Museum of Art
University of Oregon

SAM HUNT
Former student, Adjunct Professor of Art
Western Kentucky University

A MIND IN MOTION:
The Art of Charles H. Forrester

An Introductory Essay by Dr. Guy Jordan

ASSOCIATE PROFESSOR OF ART HISTORY, WESTERN KENTUCKY UNIVERSITY

IN HIS 1953 BOOK, *The Hedgehog and the Fox*, British Philosopher Isaiah Berlin described two types of thinkers. The first type, whom he termed "hedgehogs," focuses intensively on one big thing and spends their time fixated upon a singular topic or intellectual pursuit. The second type, whom he termed "foxes," knows a little about a lot of things, and spends their time making connections and drawing analogies between disparate fields of knowledge.

Charles Forrester (1928-2010) was, without a doubt, a fox—clever, creative, curious, and constantly crafting analogies between things, a master of the visual pun. His artistic projects reveal the flux and flow of an artist's mind as he mapped out correlations between experiences and synthesized something new. Forrester's material legacy—his sculptures, drawings, and scrapbooks—reveals a mind in motion, constantly linking knowledge, experience, impulses, and memories to one another through techniques that operated both at and below the level of consciousness.

Forrester's penchant for protean forms that always seem in flux between identifiable categories is apparent in some of his earliest works. His glazed teapot from 1957, for example (fig. 36), seems to oscillate before our eyes between an inert functional object and a model of a human heart, where openings and spouts mimic arteries and veins.

This anthropomorphic object formally evokes the human body and also begs to be held by someone. While the heart distributes a body's blood, Forrester's teapot distributes another kind

Fig. 36 *Glazed Tea Pot*, 1957
Ceramic clay, 8"H

of liquid ingested into the body. This rich tapestry of allusion and embodiment animates many other examples of his work. However sophisticated his interest in formal modernist compositions might have become, he never allowed his work to lose the fundamental preciousness and humanity evidenced in this teapot.

Forrester's master of fine arts thesis, completed in 1960 at the University of Oregon, comprised sculptural interpretations of the Four Evangelists (the authors attributed with creation of four Gospel accounts in the Bible's New Testament).

Charles Forrester was, without a doubt, a fox— clever, creative, curious, and constantly crafting analogies between things, a master of the visual pun.

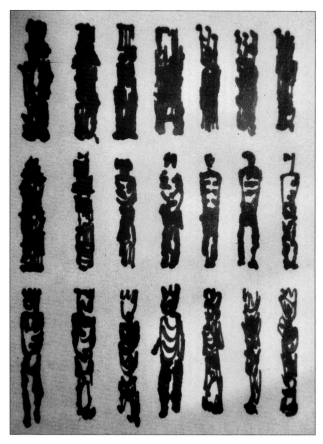

Fig. 91 ***Drawing of the Evangelist*, 1959
Felt marker drawing, 8" x 11"**

The example in this exhibition evokes Saint Matthew, which was cast five years later in 1965. The compositions of Matthew and the other three evangelists were derived from felt marker drawings (fig. 91) that evoke the spontaneity and automatic techniques of surrealist artists who were active a generation before him. He wrote in his thesis that "each drawing was done in a manner of seconds… before allowing time for the intellect to interpret the process while it was being executed." He wanted the pure structural impulses of his unconscious to govern his process, unencumbered by deliberation and choice.

Forrester trusted his sympathetic nervous system —which governs our unconscious impulses and predilections—to provide the most accurate elaboration of his true intentions as an artist. His felt drawings seem related to the flat, primal *Art Brut* figures of Jean Dubuffet, a French post-war artist who likewise preferred direct, visceral imagery. The sculpture *Evangelist–Matthew* (fig. 100, 1965, see p. 33) itself suggests a reclining abstract inchoate form, a head, spine, and perhaps a ribcage, that envelop and protect a womb-like space. The work appears frozen midway

through the process of its development. It embodies its own eternal becoming.

The sculpture does not focus on the text of that Gospel, but rather alludes to its conception and elaboration, an analogy for the creative process itself. He noted this shift from textual mediation to a more immediate way of engaging an audience in his thesis where he wrote, "In the twentieth century we have moved away from the literary world of Matthew Arnold to a new appreciation of the basic art forms which do not speak in words. Sculpture communicates with modern man in a direct, even primitive manner which defies the complexity of our times."

Forrester continued the spare, abstractly embodied directness from his early works in creative

One of the most important ingredients in Forrester's mature work is humor.

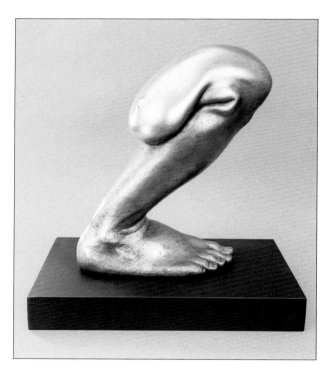

Fig. 357 *Running Abreast,* **1970**
Plaster with stain, 13"W x 4.25"D x 19"H
Forrester Family Collection

pieces such as *Vanquished* (fig. 187, 1961, see p. 32), *Fallen Warrior* (fig. 190, 1961, see p. 32), and *Seven Maidens* (fig. 237.2, 1964, see p. 79), all included in this book. These early career sculptures are like that of another major mid-century artist, the sculptor Henry Moore. Incidentally, Forrester would teach from 1963 to 1965 in Salford, UK, just an hour's drive to the southwest of Moore's hometown of Castleford. Moore, one of the most important British sculptors of the twentieth century, likewise produced abstracted

vertebrae and reclining figures organized around hollow interiors.

One of the most important ingredients in Forrester's mature work is humor. Puns abound in his art that often juxtapose seemingly incongruous forms in funny, mischievous, and thought-provoking ways.

These works show the technical skill of a master sculptor comfortable with representational work

Forrester's two-dimensional studies of high-heeled shoes are notable for their crisp art deco lines and mutability— where they often double as landscapes and reclining figures.

and abstraction. For instance, in *Running Abreast* (fig. 357, 1970), Forrester gave us a single powerful lower leg and foot topped by a female breast. The phrase "running abreast" refers to two athletes in a dead heat running side by side, where neither has a clear advantage over the other. This verbal pun was turned into a visual one where two elements that should not be connected to one another exist in a state of equilibrium. This surreal combination of a breast and a foot balances the sacred and the profane, one body part designed to nurse a child with another intended to shuffle and hop across the ground.

In a related work from the same year, *Hand Phone* (fig. 361, 1970, see p. 112), depicts

Fig. 466.3 *The Shoe as Sea & Clouds,* 1979, Pen & Ink Drawing, 6" x 8.5". **Forrester Family Collection**

a then-contemporary telephone receiver melded into a human hand. The piece begs to be touched, picked up, and held against the side of the head. In this way it engages multiple senses: vision, touch, and hearing. But if one were to actually "use" this object, the hand and fingers would cover the ear and impede rather than enhance one's ability to listen.

Forrester's works often function as visual puzzles and provocative jokes that prompt fascinating questions about the boundaries between objects and bodies. Sometimes, his visual jokes are more straightforward, such as the *Two-Headed Hammer* (fig. 542, 1986, see p. 107). Here, viewers are prompted to imagine the added efficiency (or perhaps the potential disastrous consequences,

both for the nails and one's forearm) of hammering two nails at once with an "improved" tool. Even here though, the artwork challenges the viewer to consider whether doubling an object's capabilities in fact doubles its value. Humor in Forrester's work can be deceptively instructive. Even his works that use the simplest, most direct jokes and puns provide lessons.

Perhaps shoes served as the most common subject of his work. They appear in free-standing cast sculptures, friezes, as motifs used in combination with other forms, and as the subject of many drawings, paintings, and collages.

While best known as a sculptor, his two-dimensional studies of high-heeled shoes, such as *The Shoe as Sea & Clouds* (fig. 466.3, 1979), are

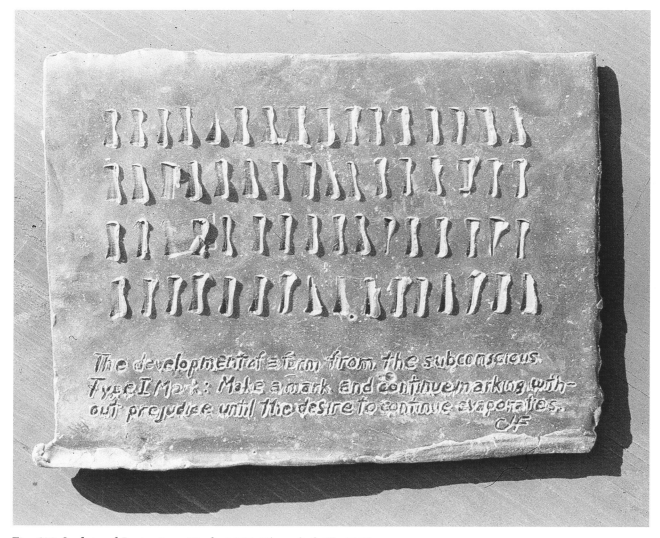

Fig. 500 *Sculptural Beginnings: Marks*, 1982, Clay relief, 6" x 7.5"

notable for their crisp art deco lines and mutability—where they often double as landscapes and reclining figures. This emphasis on the flow and flux of one form into another is a constant refrain in his work.

Forrester also investigated these themes in sculptures such as *Shoe Ship* (fig. 469, 1979, see p. 120), where a shoe and a ship meet heel-and-toe to mast and form a sailing vessel. These two forms, which ostensibly have little to do with one another, are united into a clean and polished curvilinear object that appears natural and seaworthy.

In other works, Forrester explored connections between boots and buildings, such as *Shoe as Architecture* (fig. 470, 1979, see p. 118). Both here and in *Shoe Ship,* he made a connection between an item of clothing, meant to surround and contain a single person, with vessels and structures intended to hold many people. He successfully transformed the shoe from an item of fashion into something like a monument. His work plays with the viewer's expectations and confounds their sense of scale. Is the boot as big as a Roman Temple? Or is the temple so small that it fits inside a boot? He left these relationships productively unresolved.

In a remarkable work from the early 1980s, *Sculptural Beginnings: Marks* (fig. 500, 1982), Forrester made a series of notch-like impressions on clay in a manner that recalls the cuneiform inscriptions of the Ancient Near East. Underneath these marks, he added the inscription, "The development of a form from the subconscious. Type I Mark: Make a mark and continue marking without prejudice until the desire to continue evaporates."

Forrester's written exercises, found in his scrapbooks and notebooks, reveal a similar technique. Page after page contains lists of word associations jotted down in a stream-of-consciousness fashion, one after another, until we can assume his desire to continue evaporated. He was always in search of, it seems, the perfect pun. These notebooks offer a wealth of material for those who wish to research his life and art, from profound musings about teaching objectives and the value of "folly" to column after column of pasted paper slips from fortune cookies.

On his trips and sabbaticals abroad to places like Rome, Prague, Budapest, and Istanbul, he kept detailed records of every place he ate, his daily activities, the museums and galleries he visited, and all manner of receipts. As we look upon

These volumes of thoughts and wayward distractions he clearly intended for others to see reveal a man and a mind in constant motion.

Together, with his art, they form a lasting legacy.

Charles Forrester's work in retrospection from the age of the internet, it's hard not to conceive of these books as a form of social media news feeds as he "checked in" to this or that museum, hotel, barbershop, or café. These volumes of thoughts and wayward distractions he clearly intended for others to see reveal a man and a mind in constant motion.

Together, with his art, they form a lasting legacy.

Biography

by John and Winifred Forrester

SON AND DAUGHTER OF CHARLES H. FORRESTER

IN 1928, SHORTLY before the Great Depression ravaged the United States, Charles Howard Forrester was born in Jersey City, New Jersey. Besides the widespread poverty faced by so many during that time period, Charles's family faced extreme hardship as his father, a bank accountant, served three years in prison for bank fraud. In 1932, his mother developed schizophrenia and spent her remaining years in a mental institution until her death decades later. Charles's sister, ten years older, became his caretaker and maternal figure.

World War II raged through Charles's teenage years. In New York City where he lived, Jewish refugees from Europe flooded the same ports where soldiers shipped out and dead bodies were returned home from the war front. Rumors of concentration camps in Germany spread throughout the nation, although many Americans denied the news. At the same time, Japanese-Americans were rounded up and placed in camps. The scarcity of jobs forced millions to lose their homes to foreclosure, while they also faced starvation, especially in the cities. This tumultuous backdrop imprinted itself on Charles during his youth and provided context to his later life and artwork.

After his father remarried when he was a young teenager, Charles found refuge and a welcoming home with his sister, Gay, and her new husband, Bob Worthing. When Bob got a job as a research chemist in Charleston, West Virginia, Charles moved with them. Like many New York intellectuals in the 1940s, Bob became interested in socialism and the rights of ordinary workers while he attended college. As followers of Paul Robeson, the African-American singer, actor, and political activist, the family also attended Communist Party meetings. This ultimately cost Bob his job, and it was years before he found steady employment.

In 1946, at age eighteen, Charles joined the Air Force and was stationed in South Carolina. As a radio operator, he flew in a Fairchild C-119 Flying Boxcar, a military transport aircraft. After being discharged in 1949 and earning his high

Charles knew he was talented in art and passionate about drawing, but lacked confidence to explore it as a profession.

school diploma, Charles took classes at City College in New York and received a certification from a School of Upholstery. Unfocused, he remained adrift and uncertain about his future. He knew he was talented in art and passionate about drawing, but lacked confidence to explore it as a profession.

In 1951, his fortunes changed one night at a party in New York City when he met Dorothy Reese. She was twenty-seven, engaging and educated, and had already traveled around the world. Originally from

Dorothy became Charles's muse and provided the support and encouragement he needed to explore his creativity.

Seattle, Dorothy had graduated from Barnard College in New York with a degree in political science. By 1951, she had returned from Europe after graduate study at the University of Zurich and the University of London. At twenty-two years old, Charles was a handsome rebel. When Dorothy discovered he had attended Communist Party meetings and subscribed to the *Daily Worker,* she was hooked. They married within weeks, and their loving partnership lasted fifty-three years. Dorothy became Charles's muse and provided the support and encouragement he needed to explore his creativity.

Shortly after their marriage, Charles and Dorothy moved to Seattle, where he attended the University of Washington, using the G.I. Bill. During those years, he held many part-time jobs to support his family, which included working on B-52 bomber navigation systems for Boeing. It took him seven years to graduate, as he initially studied engineering and switched to art, earning a bachelor of fine arts degree in 1958.

He studied sculpture under Everett DuPen (1912-2005), well known for his figurative sculptures. DuPen's influence is evident in Charles's work from the abstract use of the human figure in his early massive concrete sculptures to the soft curves in wood sculptures created in his later years.

Along the way, they had a child, John, and lived on a boat in Union Bay, Seattle, for several years. They spent summers living at lookout fire stations in the

Dorothy Reese Forrester, 1954.

Charles with son John aboard their sailboat, *The Chum,* in Union Bay, Seattle, 1954.

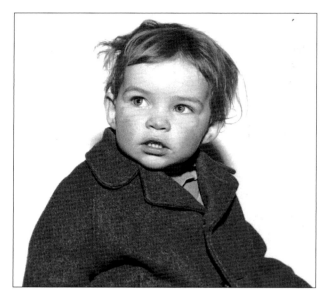

Winifred Forrester, 1960.

known as *The Equestrian* (fig. 138 see p. 75), became one of his most famous outdoor works. Sixty years later, the twenty-five-foot-tall horse and rider sculpture still stands at the west entrance to Springfield on Highway 126 as a timeless monument to the spirit of the early pioneers. Its modern abstract style caused a lot of controversy, with locals making jabs about Springfield becoming "a one-horse town." Charles held multiple community meetings during the process of building the monument. A new art movement called The Hybrids influenced his outreach as its philosophy promoted cooperation and engagement with one's local community.

By 1961, the Forrester family lived in Ashland, Oregon, where Charles continued his participation with The Hybrids movement and immersed himself in the arts community. His commissions included busts of King Lear, Malvolio, and Shylock for Oregon's Shakespearean Festival and several outdoor sculptures for the Medford Parks & Recreation Department.

The next year, restless and always looking for inspiration, he and Dorothy moved their family overseas to Florence, Italy. This move outside of the United States became one of many over the years as they traveled to foreign countries where they would live for months or even years in cheap pensions. Dorothy would use her gift of languages as an interpreter, and Charles would set up a studio and immerse himself in local architecture as inspiration to design and create sculptures. Ultimately, he and Dorothy traveled extensively across Europe, the Middle East, and the Americas for sabbaticals and residencies throughout their lifetimes.

In 1963, they moved to Manchester, England, where Charles served as a sculpture instructor at Salford Technical College (now known as the University of Salford) for the next two years. It was here that he worked with British sculptor Mike Yeomans in structural studies which inspired many of his wire

Northwest wilderness as they lived a bohemian life-style fueled by creativity and frugality—Charles built the family's furniture using plywood and black paint. While caring for her family, Dorothy immersed herself in writing and studied classic Greek and Roman literature. In 1958, the family moved to Eugene, Oregon, where their second child, Winifred, was born.

Charles studied under the internationally known artist Jan Zach at the University of Oregon with fellow sculptors Arthur Jorgenson, Walter Hannula, and Phillip Levine. Charles held a graduate teaching assistantship from 1958 to 1960, graduating with a master of fine arts degree. Zach's influence can be seen in Charles's interest in geometric lines and non-objective abstract sculpture. Other early influences were the Russian sculptor, Naum Gabo, and Buckminster Fuller. Fuller's geodesic domes inspired a generation of sculptors like Charles and New York's Kenneth Snelson with their kinetic sphere sculptures.

Early on in his career, while a graduate student, Charles began gaining notoriety for his work. In 1959, Springfield's Junior Chamber of Commerce commissioned him for a monument honoring Oregon's one-hundredth year of statehood. The sculpture, and metal tube suspended sculptures.

Just two years later, in 1965, the family moved to Southern Kentucky when Charles became the first professor of sculpture at Western Kentucky University (WKU) in Bowling Green. Dorothy, in particular, had reservations about living in the South, where schools had been recently desegregated, although racial discrimination still persisted. The need for stability and a steady paycheck won out, and Charles started teaching classes in the basement of the university's historic Cherry Hall.

Later, when the Ivan Wilson Fine Arts Center was built in 1973, Charles designed the 4,000 square-foot sculpture facility with its state-of-the-art metal casting foundries for sand casting, lost wax, and ceramic shell processes. Charles taught hundreds of students during his teaching career and was known for his tidy, well-designed studio where every tool had its place. His daily attire comprised all-black turtlenecks and pants, immune to the white plaster dust floating everywhere. He taught at WKU for the next twenty-seven years while maintaining a studio in Southern Kentucky where he created his own artwork and showed it in many galleries and exhibitions.

Charles was first introduced to the Christian Science Church by his mother during the brief early years of his life when they were together. Although the church was unable to help with her illness, the family remembered them as being kind. Years later, as an adult, Charles joined the Christian Science Church and helped to design a new building at 2033 Nashville Road in Bowling Green (now occupied by the Unitarian Universalist Church). Charles believed in the power of prayer to heal the body and rarely took medicine. He enjoyed C. S. Lewis's books and found commonality by relating his own experience of finding spirituality in religion.

Charles used Gestalt drawings for designing his sculptures, as well as modified Ouija boards

> *Charles believed in the power of prayer to heal the body and rarely took medicine.*

for creative inspiration (see sidebar in *Human Figures* category). His sculptures also reflect his intellectual curiosity of metaphysics. He read extensively about the afterlife and near-death experiences. His daughter recalls as a young teenager witnessing his ability to move small objects solely with his mind, and cannot say today with certainty whether it was a well-played ruse or if it actually happened.

Charles became an expert in many mediums, following his curiosity and love of experimenting. His large concrete outdoor sculptures are among his most well-known works, but he also created much smaller sculptures cast in bronze or aluminum using the lost wax casting technique. Charles was especially adept at working with the human figure, and he created portrait busts, as well as much larger figurative forms, in materials ranging from welded steel to laminated plywood.

Although quite capable of capturing startlingly realistic details, his works are highly stylized and often abstracted — sometimes he twisted them into sly visual puzzles and riddles. Charles's projects, as well as his kinetic sphere sculptures and wire suspension works, inspired him to take a keen interest in engineering and merge interdisciplinary processes into his already diverse creative practice.

A prolific sculptor, Charles created over five hundred fifty sculptures during his lifetime. Most have been sold to collectors. In 1992, Charles retired from teaching. Five years later, he and Dorothy moved to Nashville, Tennessee, where he maintained a studio until he died in 2010 at eighty-one.

"He was meticulous in his planning and engineering from the very beginning (for the) structural integrity of the piece, all the way to the finished surface. I never knew if Chuck was an engineer stuck in a sculptor's body or a sculptor stuck in an engineer's mind. But they always intermingled."

—RUSS FAXON, FORMER STUDENT AND SCULPTOR

The
CATEGORIES

by Joe Nolan

CHARLES HOWARD FORRESTER made 567 sculptures during his lifetime and left detailed records about each of them. The figure numbers used in the photography captions and elsewhere in the book correspond to the chronological number he assigned to each sculpture.

Early Works

YOUNG ARTISTS OFTEN EXPLORE many styles as they search for a flair of their own. These works offer insights into Forrester's early explorations where we see him working out techniques and testing materials. These early pieces also show us his initial interests in subjects, materials, and methods that came to mark his mature practice. We also see the first evidence of his love for soft, rounded forms, as well as the origins of his lifelong explorations of anatomy and architecture.

Perhaps most importantly, we see a diverse output of works that hint at a tireless curiosity and set the tone for his career. Some of the strongest examples of Forrester's early works are his portraits which demonstrate a natural knack for conveying emotion through gesture.

In *Self Portrait* (fig. 54, 1958), Forrester sees himself not unlike Auguste Rodin's *The Thinker*—the artist rests his head in his hand, and his eyes are closed in deep contemplation. He portrays himself with a bushy beard which even makes him look a little like the French master.

Waiting Woman (fig. 40, 1957) pictures its subject kneeling, her head covered in a scarf she holds together beneath her chin. Like *Self Portrait,* the *Waiting Woman* holds her eyes closed in a gesture simultaneously pained and peaceful.

Works like *Evangelist–Matthew* (fig. 100, 1965), *Vanquished* (fig. 187, 1961), and *Fallen Warrior* (fig. 190, 1961) all demonstrate Forrester's early interest in abstract works which still flirt with figuration. *Vanquished* makes use of anatomical rib-like structure, while *Fallen Warrior* echoes and includes a form like a mushroom cap.

Druid's Circle (fig. 216, 1965) offers an abstract cylindrical form that's both figurative and architectural. One can imagine the titular druids linked arm in arm in a magical circle, but the work also recalls druidic stone structures standing like Stonehenge.

Fig. 54 *Self Portrait*, 1958
Fiberglass
Steve Worthing, Asheville, NC

Fig. 40 *Waiting Woman,* 1957
Cedar wood, 24" H
Dr. W. H. Gaughan, Eugene, OR

Fig. 216 *Druid's Circle,* 1965
Bronze, 11"W x 8"D x 12.5"H
Forrester Family Collection

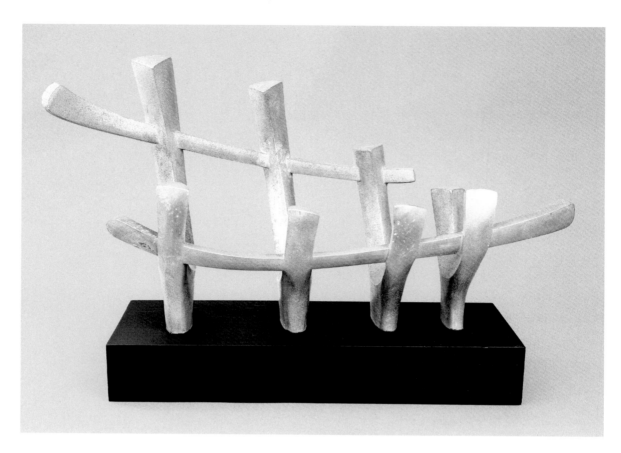

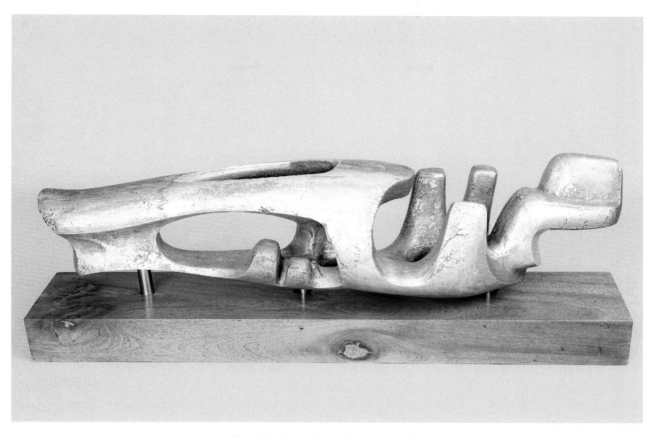

Fig. 100 *Evangelist–Matthew,* 1965
Aluminum, 31"W x 7"D x 7"H
Forrester Family Collection

Opposite page:

Above:
Fig. 187 *Vanquished,* 1961
Aluminum, 19"W x 6.5"D x 10"H
Forrester Family Collection

Below:
Fig. 190 *Fallen Warrior,* 1961
Bronze, 19.5"W x 6.5"D x 7"H
Forrester Family Collection

Human Figures

LOOKING ONLY AT FORRESTER'S human figures we can see the breadth of his works. From masterful realism to playful abstractions, these figurative pieces are the best introduction for viewers new to his art.

Comparing *The Voyage* (fig. 218, 1962) with *English Daughter* (fig. 221, 1962) we can gather insights into the broad range of expressions Forrester brought to his figurative works. *The Voyage* gives us two travelers, linking arms—they're rendered in abstract lumps and lines, their heads and facial features are jarringly geometric. We don't know if these voyagers are departing or arriving, but there is a darkness to this voyage, and I'm reminded of photographs of refugees who've had their human dignity stripped-away by war, famine, or disease. *English Daughter* gives viewers something completely different: a girl bundled-up in a winter coat, looking like she's about to head out on her morning walk to school. There is nothing abstract about this work, but it's stylized in its minimalist detailing which gives the work a buoyant joy in contrast to the darker implications of *The Voyage*.

Margo (fig. 408, 1973) and *Reclining Figure* (fig. 422, 1978) are another pair of similar, but strikingly different works. Margo finds the eponymous nude reclining into the cascade of her thick, curling hair. *Reclining Figure* is also a nude, but the body of the figure is awkwardly twisted into an unnatural position, and there is only a kind of apostrophe for a head at the end of a long neck.

Forrester also indulged his penchant for puns and hidden details in his figurative work. *Running Abreast* (fig. 357, 1970) features the lower leg of a walking figure which morphs into a single nude breast on the reverse side of the sculpture. Similarly, *Portrait Bust* (fig. 356, 1970) is a portrait of a woman's peaceful face, but the back of her head is actually another sculpture of a gracefully upturned breast.

Fig. 218 *The Voyage,* 1962
Aluminum, 14"H
J.P. Matthews & Co., North Little Rock, AR

Fig. 221 *English Daughter,* 1962
Bronze, 4.5"W x 3.75" x 17"H
Forrester Family Collection

Fig. 408 *Margo* (two views), 1973
Terracotta, 19"W x 9.5"D x 9"H
Forrester Family Collection

The Development of Sculptures from Drawings by Two People Using a Ouija Board

ARTIST'S STATEMENT BY CHARLES FORRESTER, 1978

THE *RECLINING FIGURE* (fig. 422, 1978) sculpture shown here was developed from one Ouija board drawing. The planchette was modified to accept a felt tip pen. After an initial warm-up period, the Ouija drew one picture after another, pausing only for a paper change and stopping when we decided we had enough drawings. As the eye will see only what it is capable of seeing, my students and I each interpreted the drawings differently. Some drawings were clearly mine; others had no meaning for me.

All drawings were not only transparent and showing all edges at once, but they presented different sculptures from different views. The problem was to redraw them as a solid sculptural object.

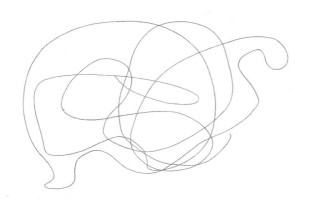

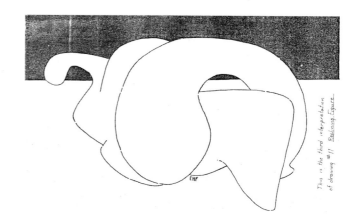

Fig. 422 *Reclining Figure,* 1978
Bronze, 12"W x 5.5"D x 4.5"H
Forrester Family Collection

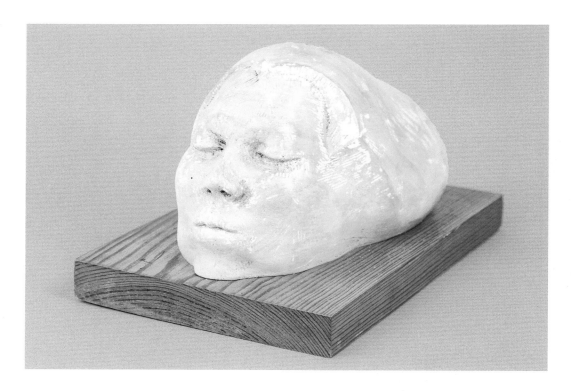

Fig. 356 *Portrait Bust,* **1970**
Plaster with stain, 9.25"W x 6"D x 6.5"H
Forrester Family Collection

Fig. 357 *Running Abreast,* **1970**
Plaster with stain, 13"W x 4.25"D x 19"H
Forrester Family Collection

Portrait Busts

FORRESTER'S PORTRAIT BUSTS offer another example of his eye for realistic detailing and his capacity for capturing likenesses. No matter the subject, Forrester's love of soft forms and dynamic curving lines is often present. That said, there are also plenty of diverse stylistics on display in these works which, for all of their similarities, each stand alone as unique expressions of his masterful hand.

Across Forrester's oeuvre we rarely see a missed opportunity for punning, humor, or playing the trickster. Obviously, Forrester was a serious artist, but his work is thoroughly infused with a sense of humor and a love of play. With his portrait busts, Forrester's sly sleight of hand can be found in his materials themselves.

Forrester's *King Lear* (fig. 162, 1961) imagines one of Shakespeare's greatest characters with a receding hairline, a heavy brow, and a long, full beard. It looks like Forrester, fittingly, carved this striking, regal portrait out of stone. But in fact, this piece is actually cast using a concrete masonry form of artificial stone.

The bust *Mrs. Darling* (fig. 338.1, 1969) was modeled from a Jerry's Restaurant waitress that the Forresters befriended, and *Howard Gettis Forrester* (fig. 367, 1971) was Forrester's father. These two works appear to be cast in bronze, but they're actually plaster with black shoe polish and gold paint applied to mimic a shiny metallic surface.

But for all of the hijinks at hand here, Forrester's busts are also a testament to his ability to evoke the likeness of his subjects with just the slightest details: an upturned corner of the mouth, a pensive lidded gaze, the tight knot of scarf, or an unruly lock of hair.

These works were produced throughout Forrester's career, many through private or institutional commissions. *King Lear* was created for the Oregon Shakespeare Festival, while *President Dero Downing, Western Kentucky University* (fig. 517, 1983) can be found today at Jody Richards Hall on campus, along with four other commissioned WKU presidents' busts crafted by Forrester.

Fig. 162 *King Lear,* 1961
Cast stone, Life-size bust
Oregon Shakespeare Festival, Ashland, OR

Fig. 318 *Madrian Lee,* 1966
Plaster, Life-size bust

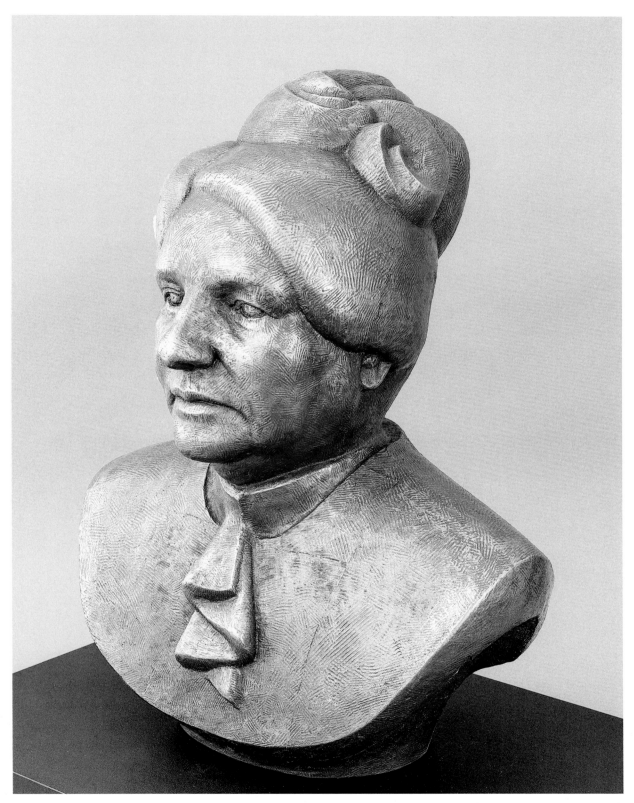

Fig. 338.1 *Mrs. Darling,* 1969
Plaster, 15"W x 10.5"D x 21"H
Forrester Family Collection

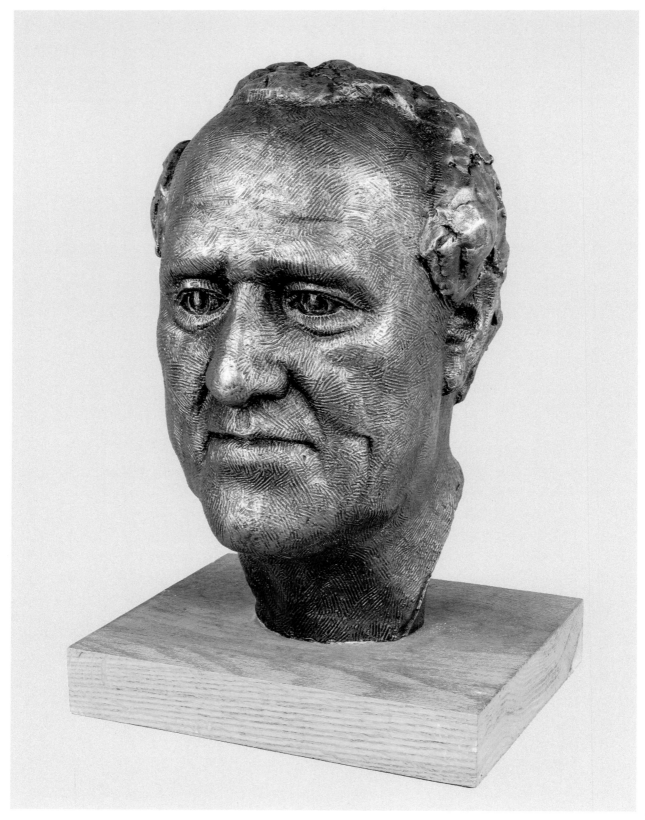

Fig. 367 *Howard Gettis Forrester,* 1971
Plaster, 8"W x 9.5"D x 13.5"H
Forrester Family Collection

Fig. 517 *President Dero Downing, Western Kentucky University,* **1983**
Plaster, 18.75"H
Western Kentucky University

Bronze and Other Mediums

THESE WORKS SHOW Forrester's range with his smaller sculptures from figurative to biomorphic to architectural. His voluptuous forms and stylized lines are recognizably present regardless of medium or technique.

Works like *Space Fungas* (fig. 331, 1967) and *Departure II* (fig. 353, 1970) reflect Forrester's most experimental and cosmic side. *Space Fungas* is a pale, lugubrious form that appears to be dripping down the edges of a pedestal in large, pendulous blobs. Here Forrester played with materiality itself and challenged ideas about what viewers typically expect from a finished sculptural form. *Space Fungas* doesn't give us an idealized shape or figure. Instead, it offers lines and textures in a state of flux—a composition in transition.

Departure II is another abstract form defined by curtain-like folds and a series of outcroppings at the top of the sculpture that seem vaguely architectural—like a row of chimneys or small towers. Smooth and bulbous sections are balanced against lines and textures that are sharp and angular.

With works like *The Back Side* (fig. 304, 1966), *Squatting Woman* (fig. 370, 1978), and *Legacy* (fig. 400, 1972), Forrester balanced his approach between figuration and abstraction. *Legacy* takes elements of a face—an eye, nose, and lips—but separates them into a cubist arrangement in an architectural setting composed of pillars and steps. At first glance, *The Back Side* looks like a mushroom sprouting from the hollow of a tree stump, represented by a graceful bowl-like shape that cradles the sprouting fungus in a smooth, rounded space defined by undulating feminine lines. Viewed from the opposite angle, the titular "back side" comes into view in the form of a shapely woman's buttocks. *The Back Side* offers two separate concepts, two sculptures in one.

Squatting Woman is similar, but more subtle. From certain angles, Forrester's minimal detailing and the textured surface of the piece make it appear as a vaguely feminine, but abstract, form composed of smooth, curving spaces and lines. Upon continued inspection, fingers and toes come into view. While the thick limbs and extreme posture are stylized and exaggerated, this is a figurative work, but one that's playfully indirect.

Forrester's *The Broom Man* (fig. 567, 2000)—a portrait of an eccentric East Nashville street performer he befriended—was one of his last works, completed in 2000.

Fig. 331 *Space Fungas,* 1967
Polyester resin, 81"H

Fig. 304 *The Back Side* (two views), 1966
Terracotta, 9.5"W x 8"D x 11"H
Forrester Family Collection

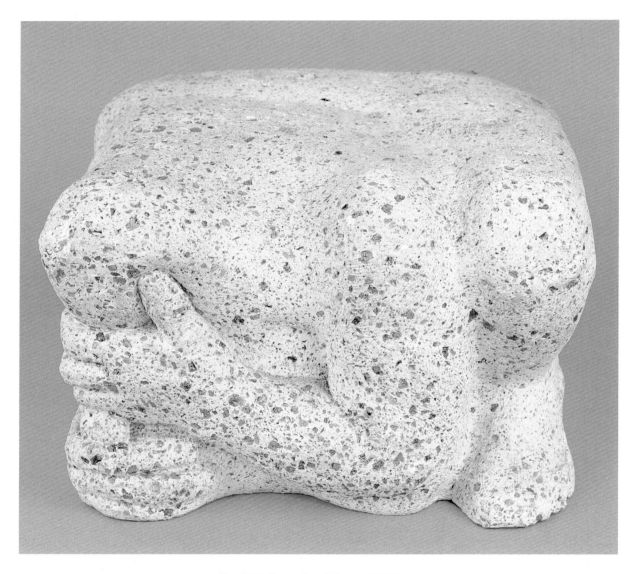

Fig. 370 *Squatting Woman,* 1978
Plaster & zonolite, 9"W x 11"D x 8"H
Forrester Family Collection

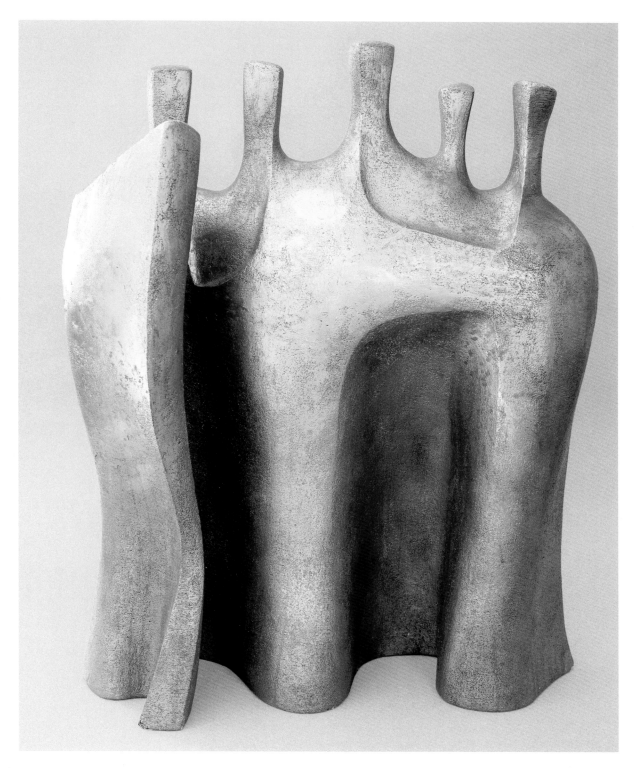

Fig. 353 *Departure II,* 1970
Terracotta, 19"W x 8"D x 25"H
Forrester Family Collection

Fig. 400 *Legacy*, 1972
Terracotta, 13"W x 13"D x 18.75"H
Forrester Family Collection

The Broom Man

By Winifred Forrester

THE FORRESTERS FREQUENTLY enjoyed long afternoons socializing in coffee shops or restaurants. They often made friends with strangers and were interested in learning about their lives and daily struggles.

They moved to East Nashville in 1998, a few months after a mile-wide tornado sowed destruction through their neighborhood. In 2000, Forrester befriended a man at one of his local haunts, the McDonald's on Gallatin Pike.

Much to his family's dismay, he invited him home. Family members were concerned, observing he was unpredictable and eccentric. Nevertheless, he fascinated Forrester, who wanted him to model for a sculpture.

Forrester had seen him featured in a photograph on the front page of the local newspaper, *The Tennessean*. As an impromptu street performer who strummed a broom like a guitar at the Summer Lights Festival, he earned the nickname, The Broom Man.

Forrester convinced The Broom Man to model for him, and as it turned out, this was one of his last sculptures. Forrester had been diagnosed with Parkinson's disease and passed away in 2010.

Fig. 567 *The Broom Man,* 2000
Bronze, 7"W x 7.5"D x 27"H
Forrester Family Collection

Creation of a Bronze Sculpture

LOST WAX CASTING PROCESS

by Russ Faxon, Sculptor, Bell Buckle, Tennessee

THE TECHNIQUE OF LOST WAX BRONZE CASTING has been used for thousands of years with little changes to the actual method. The traditional bronze metal mixture contains mostly copper, with smaller amounts of other metals. The process allows for precise replication, and results in artwork that is extremely durable and long-lasting.

Creating a bronze sculpture begins with developing an original model generally in clay, wood, or stone, which will later be transformed into wax. Once the model is complete, a rubber mold is created around it to capture every detail. The rubber mold is then removed from the original model and put back together, leaving a hollow cavity or negative of the original. Hot wax is poured into the hollow cavity and then poured back out, leaving a hollow wax copy inside. The wax duplicate is then removed from the rubber mold, and seam lines and imperfections are repaired.

Following this process, a sprueing system made of wax rods is attached to strategic points of the wax figure to allow the bronze to flow into the sculpture. The wax rods are attached to a wax cup which will serve as the pouring container for the bronze. A ceramic shell mold is made around the wax figure and placed in a fiery furnace which melts the wax away, leaving a hollow cavity to receive the bronze. The name "Lost Wax Casting" was derived from the loss or melting of the wax.

Two thousand degree molten bronze is then poured into the ceramic shell mold to recreate every detail of the wax model. After twenty-four hours, when the bronze has cooled sufficiently, the shell mold is carefully broken off with a hammer to reveal the casting. The sprues are cut off, and a labor-intensive repair process called "metal chasing" is performed. After all imperfections are ground down, it is then cleaned, and acid patina is applied to give the sculpture color. The sculpture is then sealed with wax to protect and highlight the color, after which the sculpture is mounted to an appropriate base.

Each figure reproduction must be recreated in wax from the original rubber mold, derived from the original clay figure. Though a time-consuming process, the final product, even for reproductions, becomes a unique and timeless piece of art.

Drawings and Paintings

INSPIRED BY ANCIENT RUINS and classical architecture, these drawings and paintings were a product of Forrester's sabbatical in Italy and Greece from 1978 to 1979. Drawing plays an intrinsic role in the process of sculpture making, but the pieces in this category are their own works of art.

The word "brummagem" is an alteration of the English city, Birmingham. The word dates back to the seventeenth century when Birmingham became notorious as a locale that specialized in minting counterfeit coins, cheap trinkets, and costume jewelry. Forrester's *The Brummagem Shoe* (fig. 467.8, 1979) is a fun exploration of the common space shared by drawing and sculpture. This drawing is dramatically asymmetrical with the titular glamorous high-heeled shoe just beginning to make a stage right exit from the picture. The sexy, curving lines of the stepping shoe and the chic grayscale palette make this one appear like a particularly eye-catching advertising illustration. But Forrester decorated his shoe in a thick coat of silver glitter and managed to transform a material that's emblematic of tackiness into a startling expression of texture.

Shoe as Puzzle (fig. 467.7, 1979) is a slyly sophisticated and complex work which shares its high-heeled form with *The Brummagem Shoe.* But this shoe is rendered in a series of numbered dots instead of black lines and glitter. This "connect the dots" presentation is another example of how Forrester often hid figures and forms in his work, rewarding viewers' deeper attention and willingness to interact with these pieces.

Shoe as Puzzle literally asks viewers to fill-in-the-blank for themselves. It's a surreptitiously psychedelic work that presents a straightforward image, but also reflects on the viewer's perception and the process of seeing. *Shoe Lace* (fig. 472.1, 1979) embraces design aesthetics, reiterating Forrester's high-heeled shoe form in a column of shoe shapes paired in mirror images. The repetitive images create a primitive-seeming pattern of Northwestern Native American designs.

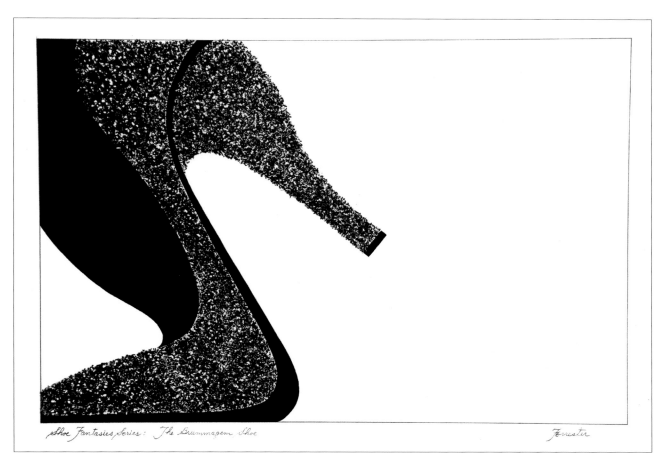

Shoe Fantasies Series: The Brummagem Shoe   Forrester

Fig. 467.8 *The Brummagem Shoe,* 1979
Gouache & glitter, 15" x 20"
Forrester Family Collection

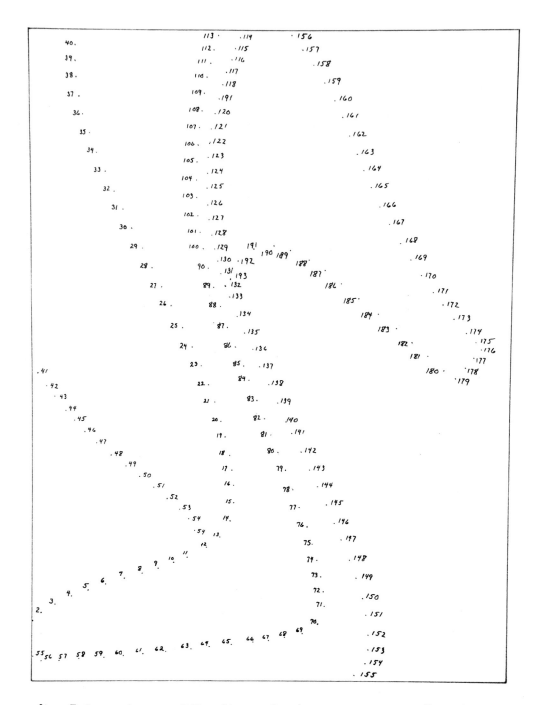

Shoe Fantasies Series: 467 Shoe as Puzzle   Forrester

Fig. 467.7 *Shoe as Puzzle,* **1979**
Pen & ink drawing, 15" x 20"
Forrester Family Collection

Shoe Fantasies Series: 470   For Sale to Tourists   Forrester

Fig. 470.5 *For Sale to Tourists*, 1979
Pen & ink drawing, 15" x 20"
Forrester Family Collection

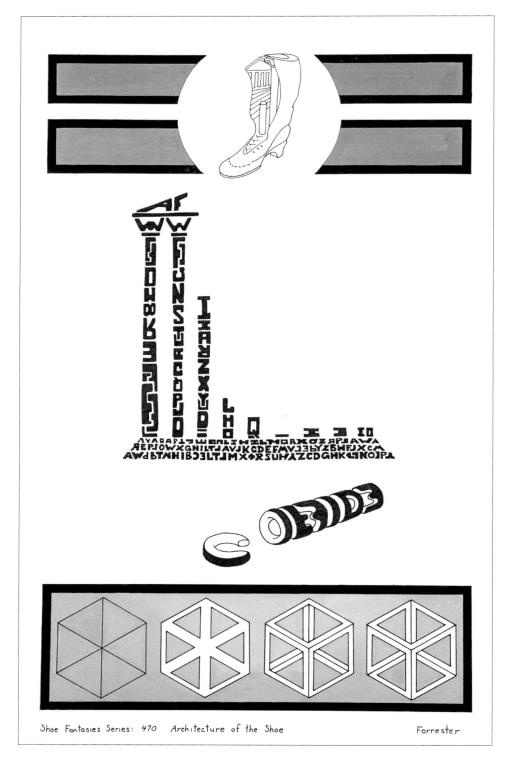

Shoe Fantasies Series: 470   Architecture of the Shoe   Forrester

Fig. 470.1 *Architecture of the Shoe,* **1979**
Tempera painting, 15" x 20"
Forrester Family Collection

Fig. 469.1 *Shoe Ship,* **1979**
Tempera painting, 15" x 20"
Forrester Family Collection

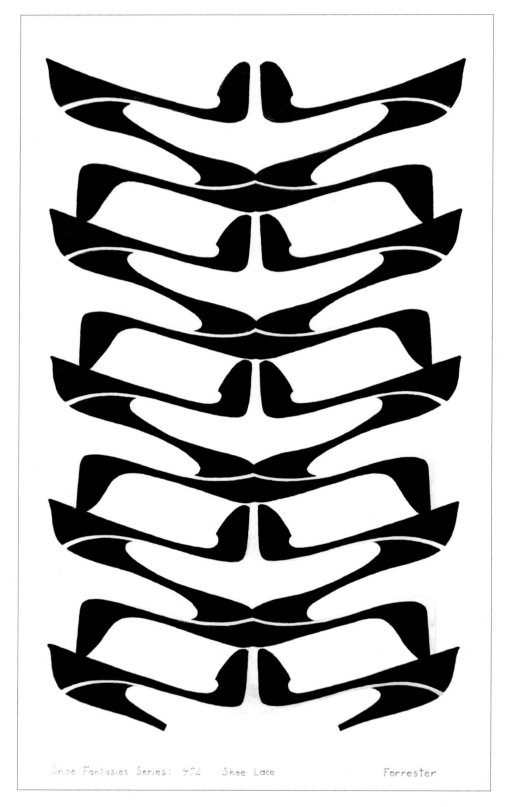

Fig. 472.1 *Shoe Lace,* **1979**
Tempera painting, 15" x 20"
Forrester Family Collection

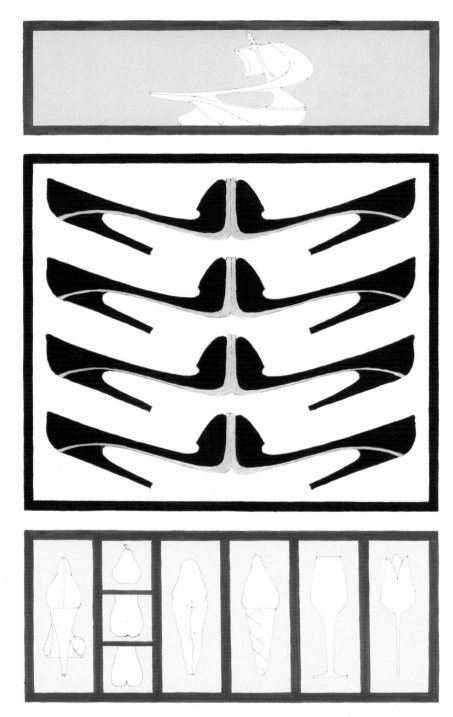

Fig. 479.5 *Shoe as Related Form I,* **1979**
Tempera painting, 15" x 20"
Forrester Family Collection

Laminated Plywood

BETWEEN 1985 AND 1992, after a sabbatical in Prague, Czechoslovakia, Forrester created a series of works using plywood. Used in interior design, this material originated as an artistic form in the 1940s with Charles and Ray Eames in their furniture making. Forrester elevated this common building supply into singular works of fine art, which have become textural treasures. This medium allowed him to realize his unmistakably stylized figures while also nodding at their playful deconstruction.

This new medium inspired Forrester to create a wide variety of female portraits along with the occasional animal form. *Martha III* (fig. 547, 1988) is emblematic of these works, which feature full forms defined by graceful lines, but only the most minimal detailing. *Martha III* twists sideways—her hair falls over one shoulder and her arms are slightly bent. It appears that one of her legs is also slightly bent and she's standing on the ball of her foot as if about to execute a complete turn. But Forrester has frozen her in space and given viewers only the minimum of specifics—her legs are covered by her long dress, her arms are rectangular and undefined, her blank face holds no features. This less-is-more approach forces viewers to take in the overall form of the work and to notice the infinite textural complexities in the striated planes of the laminated material.

Another female figure is slightly more detailed with a more dynamic pose. *Sybil II Swinger* (fig. 549, 1989) wears a strapless dress with a dramatic profile, but again, Forrester left many of the details for viewers to fill in, which results in highlighting the sculpture's material.

With *The Raven* (fig. 554, 1990), the stylized approach still applies—the simple detailing resembles the hawk imagery we find in Egyptian hieroglyphs. The bird's shape is exaggerated—squat and thick—but the tips of its wings are so delicately defined they appear to dance at the edges of the block where it is perched.

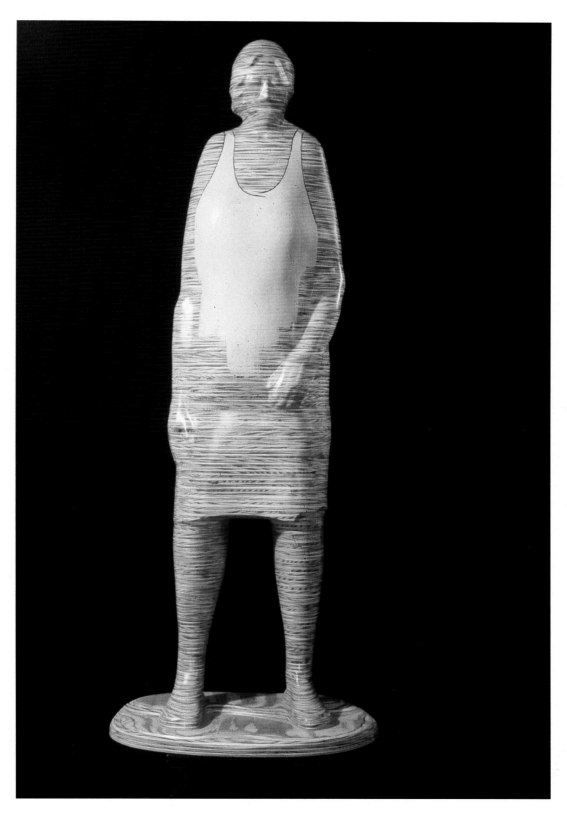

Fig. 553 *Lady in Blue II,* 1990
Laminated wood, 56.5"H
Casey Lester, Bowling Green, KY

Making Martha II

THE MULTI-STEP PROCESS of creating *Martha II* (fig. 529, 1985), a nine-foot-tall laminated maple wood sculpture:

Commissioned by Northern Telecom in 1985, *Martha II* was installed at their offices in Nashville, Tennessee. Its current location is unknown as the company filed for bankruptcy protection in 2009.

The hand-crafted process for laminated plywood art is laborious and requires extensive technical expertise. Forrester devoted hours to planning the process from start to finish. Hand sketches were made to design the sculpture's shape. Then, he created a small plaster maquette which served to guide the final form. Next, paper templates were created by hand, precisely measured and cut for each layer without using 3D modeling software. The layers of ¾" plywood were stacked, creating a step effect. Each layer was meticulously measured, numbered, and cut. Then the individual layers were glued and clamped together constructing the approximated solid form.

In the case of *Martha II,* two large sections were made separately due to the significant size and weight of the overall sculpture. This aided in its transport and installation. The surface edges were trimmed with power and hand tools to carve and sand it into finished shape. The final step applied several finish coats of oil.

Fig. 547 *Martha III,* 1988
Laminated wood, 45"H
Collection of U.S. Bank

Opposite page:
Fig. 529 *Martha II,* 1985
Laminated wood, 9'H
Northern Telecom Commission

Fig. 549 *Sibyl II Swinger* (two views), 1989
Laminated wood, 11"W x 11.5"D x 53"H
Forrester Family Collection

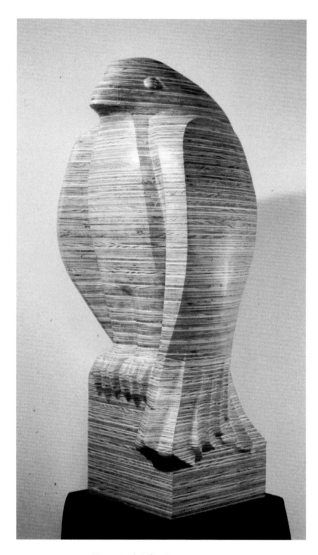

Fig. 554 *The Raven,* **1990**
Laminated wood, 45"H
US Bank, Bowling Green, KY

Right:
Fig. 548 *Martha IV,* **1989**
Laminated wood, 67"H
Eskind Family Collection, Nashville, TN

Outdoor Sculpture

FORRESTER'S OUTDOOR SCULPTURES unearth his signature curves and dynamic lines translating to monumental scale. These large scale works are among his best known.

His Pacific Northwest connections led to his first monumental sculpture commission, *The Equestrian* (fig. 138, 1959), in Springfield, Oregon. This massive depiction of horse and rider was dedicated in 1960 to celebrate Oregon's centennial. Forrester exaggerated the horse's massive haunches as it descends toward viewers in a dramatic downward angle. The rider raises his right hand in a grand salute. Forrester gave us minimal detailing. The lines where the rider meets the horse and the horse meets the landscape were purposely left undefined. They are all connected. They are all one.

The Equestrian helped to define Forrester's early career and set the stage for the large works to come. Works like *Family* (fig. 217, 1975) bear a striking resemblance to *The Equestrian.*

Not surprisingly, Forrester's large scale works are as diverse as his smaller pieces. They vary from an architectural outdoor wooden playground constructed in Oregon to the abstracted figures found in the *Seven Maidens* (fig. 237.2, 1964), installed at the Broughton Girls' High School in Salford, England. The English location of the latter is noteworthy because of the *Seven Maidens'* resemblance to Forrester's other works like *Druid's Circle* (fig. 216, 1965, see p. 31), which directly references the ancient monumental architecture that decorates numerous locations across Great Britain.

Fig. 148 *Evangelist,* **1959**
Concrete, Est. 12'H

The Equestrian

by Caroline Phillips
EUROPEAN & AMERICAN ART CURATORIAL EXTERN
JORDAN SCHNITZER MUSEUM OF ART, EUGENE, OREGON

AS A YOUNG GRADUATE student at the University of Oregon, Charles Forrester would create one of his most famous public art sculptures, *The Equestrian* (fig. 138).

In 1959 the Springfield Junior Chamber of Commerce sought submissions for a monument to commemorate the centennial of Oregon's statehood. A testament to his early promise as a sculptor, the committee selected Forrester's design for a twenty-five-foot-tall horse and rider, which stood out among a field of designs by established artists.

Positioned at the western entrance to Springfield on Highway 126, the sculpture reimagines the traditional equestrian statue formula. Rather than presenting a highly refined, naturalistic horse, Forrester was interested in the possibilities of form on a monumental scale. At the time, some Springfield residents were concerned about the legibility of such abstraction and hoped instead for a more naturalistic image of a local logger or fisherman. Yet, Forrester had the foresight to design a monument to Oregon that would stand the test of time.

In the contentious community meetings held over several months, Forrester faced criticism with a measured response. He defended abstraction and the charge that he should sculpt a naturalistic rendering of a horse. He insisted on the generative possibilities of abstraction. Indeed, the formal continuity between base, horse, and rider draws attention to the negative space of the monument. Eschewing minute details such as the horse's mane or the rider's features, Forrester put the lush evergreen setting into dialogue with the massive white form.

Forrester's vision prevailed and in May 1959, he began to work on the internal support for the sculpture. He constructed the iron rod framework in the sculpture studio at the University of Oregon. However, the ceiling of the studio was only sixteen feet high, so he built the frame in two parts and assembled the frame on-site in August 1959. There, he began to pour the concrete, and by October of that year, he completed the sculpture. After the sculpture was installed, the controversy over naturalism or abstraction faded away. Today, Forrester's work has become part of the fabric of the community and has earned the admiration of its residents.

Fig. 138 *The Equestrian,* **1959, with young John Forrester**
Concrete, 25'H
Springfield, OR

Fig. 184 *Hawthorn Park Outdoor Playground,* **1961, with young Winifred Forrester**
Wood, Est. 6'H
Hawthorn Park, Medford, OR

Fig. 217 *Family*, 1975
Concrete, 9'H
Hospital Hill, Bowling Green, KY

FORRESTER SAVED NUMEROUS critiques of his work, and perhaps the most interesting one is a letter written to him in 1964 about the *Seven Maidens* public art in Salford, England:

March 11, 1964

Dear Mr. Forrester,

Given a cement mixer I too could create 7 young girls as you portray them. Obviously any illiterate fool could do the same because the dictionary does explain sculpture-noun—art of forming figures in relief or solid; product of this art- v.t. represent by sculpture. Now have you seen anything like that walking about lately? Not even in a nightmare I feel sure.

I suggest you try to copy something in life, a schoolgirl for instance. Any bets it's an impossibility for you?

Art is defined in the dictionary as a noun and means skill but it does also say craft, contrivance, cunning, trick—all of these things are what you are expert at. Thus you are the type that contaminates minds (plural noun) by making something which is non-existent. Thus I feel sure a psychiatrist could help you.

Sincerely, Miss P. Mills

Forrester, along with Miss Audrey Winstanley and Miss Maria Frederick, secretaries presumably with the Broughton Girls' High School, admiring *Seven Maidens*.

Fig. 237.2 *Seven Maidens,* 1964
Cast stone, 7'H
Broughton Girls' High School, Salford, England

Welded Steel

FORRESTER'S WORKS in welded steel are testaments to texture. These figures and forms are notable for their graceful transformations of unyielding materials.

Abstractions of familiar figures and forms, these works seem almost liberated by this hard, heavy substance. Forrester created pieces packed with sharp, angular lines and details that stand in direct contrast to the rounded forms and more minimal detailing that defines so many of his signature works.

Two pieces dedicated to Gospel authors offer the best examples: *Study for Evangelist –Luke* (fig. 98, 1959) pictures the disciple with his arms folded—his head is covered in a crown-like tassel of hair, and he's taking a jaunty step forward, off to spread the Good News. Forrester constructed the figure using uniform, repetitive rows of small steel rods to define the limbs, torso, and head. The results of this method appear both raw and immediate, strict and stately. There is an inherent drama in this precise arrangement of unfinished materials. Even though this figure is made up of heavy, dense parts, the lines and gestures Forrester used make this statue look light on its feet.

Evangelist–St. John (fig. 99, 1959) was also constructed from many small pieces of steel. But here Forrester used an almost cubist approach, fleshing out this biblical author with multitudes of small metal plates joined together at odd angles. Parts of the structure are intrinsic to the design of this life-sized construction, but many of the plates seem added purely for decorative quality. The end result reveals an imposing work that resembles a black suit of armor and nods to Alberto Giacometti's long, lean, textured figures. These Bible-inspired works were completed in the late 1950s, very early in Forrester's career.

A decade later, works like *Leaves* (fig. 330, 1966) found the ever-restless Forrester marrying minimalist metal forms into multimedia art hangings bound with twine. *One Person on a Bench* (fig. 327.3, 1968) completes the welded steel category with a nod to his love of the human form.

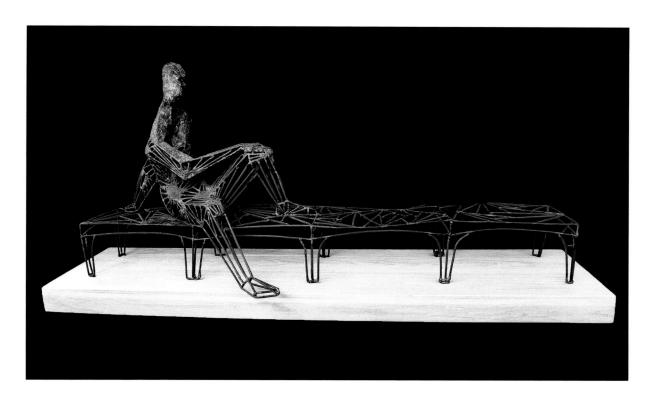

Above:
Fig. 327.3 *One Person on a Bench,* **1968**
Welded iron wire, 39.5"W x 11.375"D x 18"H
Forrester Family Collection

Right:
Fig. 330 *Leaves,* **1966**
Iron wire & twine, 3 strands of 50", 52" & 37"
Forrester Family Collection

The Hybrids
ANYTHING OF HETEROGENEOUS ORIGIN OR COMPOSITION
By Winifred Forrester

IN EUGENE, OREGON, Forrester was associated with a new art movement, The Hybrids, which emphasized cooperation among the arts.

They did not believe the artist should hide in a garret; rather the artist's new role should be to enter society and "become an immediate and positive witness for his art in his community," according to their declaration. The Hybrids' declaration also said, "We pronounce dead the era in which the artist concerned himself with perfecting form as a bulwark against materialism."

Forrester and The Hybrids believed all artists, including sculptors, painters, architects, weavers, and metalworkers, should combine their efforts to include the masses, and not just for a few private patrons.

The Hybrids' first collective exhibition was at the University of Oregon's Museum of Art in 1959. Forrester's selection was *Evangelist–St. John* (fig. 99, 1959). His artist's statement from the exhibit stated, "This represents my belief in depth as a basic element of form in sculpture. Here I have attempted to divide mass from volume, but depth remains and is indivisible. I would describe sculpture as an activation of space which leads to a mystical reality. My interpretation of sculpture is offered not as a negation of the past but rather a growth based on the past and orientated toward the future."

In the forward for the exhibit program, Jan Zach, the university's resident sculptor stated, "The work of an artist consists of an unprejudiced search for the solution which symbolizes for him the phenomena of daily life. His work is basically important for a real democracy and for a unification of aims. I am confident only in teamwork for the intensification of the cultural component. As always, the spark which puts life in a movement originates in the creative mind of an individual, but only with close work together in the team, in the interchange of ideas and in serious criticism, are constructive works of importance achieved."

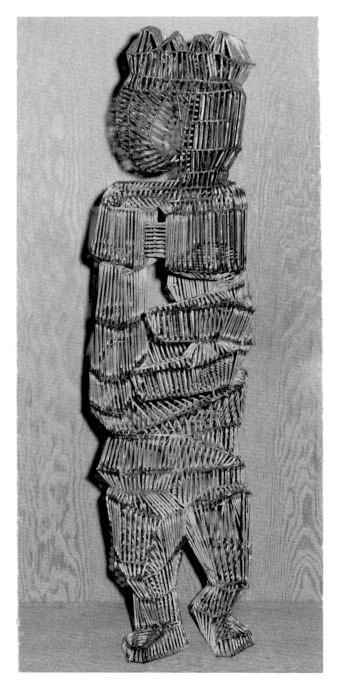

Fig. 98 *Study for Evangelist–Luke,* **1959**
Welded wire, 36"H

Opposite page:
Fig. 99 *Evangelist–St. John,* **1959,**
with Forrester and artwork admirer
Steel Plate, 7'H

Wire Suspension

FORRESTER'S EXPERIMENTS with wire suspension yielded some of his most sublime works. Completed in the 1960s and 1970s, these striking forms are feats of engineering as well as pieces of art.

They mark a decade and a half during which Forrester moved to Bowling Green, Kentucky, to teach at Western Kentucky University, where he served as a professor for nearly thirty years. During that time, Forrester traveled to Canada, Austria, England, Spain, Italy, Greece, and Yugoslavia, gathering the experiences and inspirations that fueled his mid-career.

Space Probe (fig. 215, 1963) is a column made up of abstract elements. It simultaneously recalls the indigenous art of the American Northwest and captures the spirit of the "Space Race" between America and the Soviet Union during the 1960s. One-part ritual object, one-part aspirational monument, this work is visually striking, but it also boasts an ingenious design which finds the work suspended from itself in a feat of cast metal, wire, tension, and balance.

Admirality Blue & Gold Sphere (fig. 438, 1978) and *The Blue Sphere* (fig. 434, 1978) were both inspired by Buckminster Fuller's dome designs, as well as NASA's Apollo lunar module which landed the first astronauts on the moon in 1969. *Admirality Blue & Gold Sphere* is a small sculpture of steel tubes and wires in the titular palette. It reads like the little brother to *The Blue Sphere,* which is ten-and-a-half feet tall and features a kinetic swash of shiny, curved steel plates decorating the steel tubes and wires. Impressively, this whole structure can be broken down and folded into a single small box in a feat that Fuller himself would have admired.

Fig. 215 *Space Probe,* 1963
Aluminum, 8'H
Kentucky Museum
Bowling Green, KY

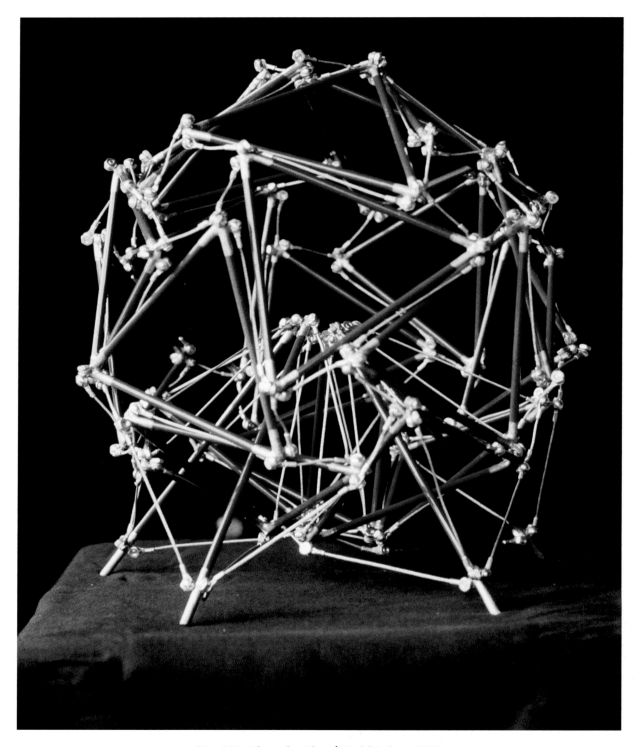

Fig. 438 *Admiralty Blue & Gold Sphere*, 1978
Steel tube & wire, 16"H
J. Mondole

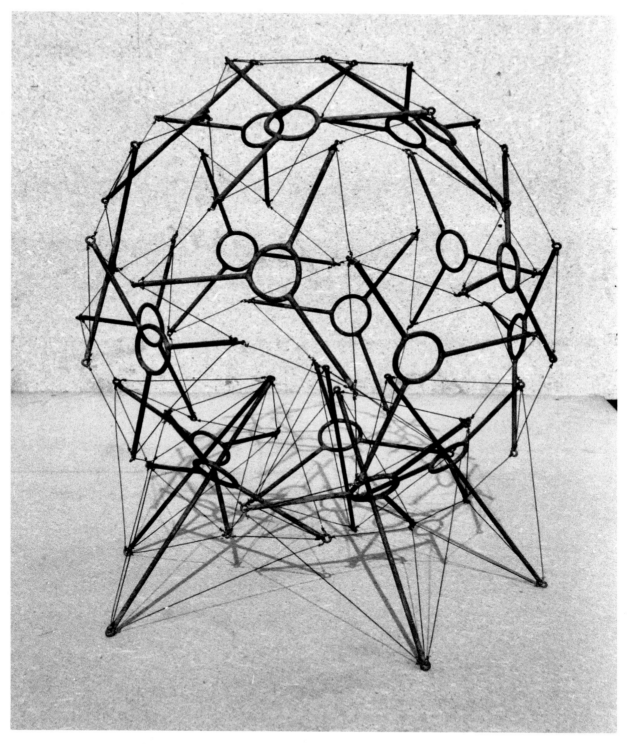

Fig. 261 *Gooseberry,* **1964**
Iron & piano wire, Est. 36"H
Charles Roberts, Bowling Green, KY

The Blue Sphere

By Sam Hunt, Adjunct Professor of Art, Western Kentucky University

AS A FRESHMAN IN 1974, I first walked into the ground floor sculpture studio of Western Kentucky University's Fine Arts Building and into Charles Forrester's extraordinary world. There was a place for every conceivable tool with its silhouette outlined on the wall, like the brand on a cow. The studio was home to the messiest of processes, yet it was gleaming and spotless. For the next four years it became my adopted home.

As I ended my undergraduate work, Mr. Forrester asked me to apprentice with him. I was to help enlarge one of his earlier sculptural prototypes, a large blue sphere. The sphere consisted of a number of triangular-shaped panels formed from metal piping. My job was to manufacture the panels. His job was to create the cabling systems used to levitate these panels independently of one another, suspending them to form a huge sphere. When assembled, it looked similar to an exploding Buckminster Fuller sphere with moving parts.

As I began work on the panels, I had mixed emotions. I was overjoyed at seeing his creative process from the inside and petrified knowing that one tiny error, on my part, and the piece wouldn't work. I needn't have worried. He was the brain, and I was the grunt. I wouldn't be allowed to fail. The sculpture was like the studio – it was designed and redesigned within an inch of its existence before actual construction ever began. My first step was cutting pipe. Every pipe had to be exactly the same. He made a jig for that. Then, I had to collapse and flatten exactly two inches of the pipes. No problem, another jig. To drill two holes in exactly the right spot, you got it, another jig. Yet another was devised to bend each end of the pipe to the exact angle needed to create a perfect equilateral triangle, by bolting three pipes together. Most sculptors would have been proud to place one of those jigs on a pedestal as art.

After a week of making panels and Mr. Forrester making cabling, we were ready to float the sphere. We began in the studio's plaster room, attaching cables, adding one panel at a time, until, slowly, a large bowl of triangles appeared. We added more. It was almost there. I remember us both collapsing in exhausted laughter as we realized the sphere was too big for the room. We were going to have to take it apart and build it all again, outside. I never worked so hard or enjoyed work more.

Like most of his sculptures, *The Blue Sphere* (fig. 434, 1978) was designed to be shipped from place to place for display. He engineered wooden crates for many of his sculptures. Inside, were storage spaces for each component, and each compartment was arranged in such a way as to leave no empty, unused space inside the crate. This eliminated the need for any kind of padded packing materials and ensured the crate was as small as possible. Many times, the shipping/storage crate was designed to become the display pedestal for the sculpture stored inside. Like his jigs, these storage boxes were never afterthoughts. They were always painted and decorated with his signature "Folly" logo. The interiors were always labeled and mapped to facilitate speedy assembly and inventory of the sculpture's components. Art within art, like nesting Russian dolls.

Fig. 434 *The Blue Sphere,* 1978
Steel tube & wire, 10'6"H

The Blue Sphere in its storage box,
engineered to maximize space.

Mixed Media

FORRESTER'S MIXED MEDIA WORKS range from minimal monuments to magically mismatched machines. These works find the artist in his most playful state.

Ninety Degrees (fig. 339, 1969) is a spiraling wood and cardboard tower. A red cube at the base and another at the top are separated by a twisting column of thick cardboard layers. He used the material to achieve an abstract architectural form instead of a figurative one. Simple in design, *Ninety Degrees* has chic lines and the bold pop of red color that make this one as sexy as it is sophisticated. It's a unique piece among works which tend to mimic machines and musical instruments.

Forrester's mixed media pieces are found object works he built by borrowing bits from musical instruments, audio, electrical, automotive, and plumbing equipment and supplies. These works showcase his playful side, but they also demonstrate his understanding of mechanics and design—it's not clear what these works might do, but the way they're made makes them appear like real working objects.

Zappo L'Art Trompeur (fig. 514, 1983) is aptly named by including the French phrase "L'Art Trompeur" meaning a misleading work of art. It looks like a mix between a desk mic, vintage telephone, and movie film camera. It could also be a medical device. The institutional black really sells this work as an important piece of equipment in an industry from another world capable of zapping someone.

Whistles and Bells (fig. 515, 1983) looks like something a character in a Dr. Seuss drawing might play. Whistles, the bell of a horn, a metal tank, and a pink plastic wheel all combine to make viewers imagine the bizarre sounds this thing might create if only somebody knew how to play it.

Collages and assemblages work best when the results are greater than the sum of their parts, and Forrester's best mixed media art manages to transform bits and pieces into fantastical, magical objects packed with beauty, humor, and ideas.

Fig. 339 *Ninety Degrees,* 1969
Wood & cardboard, 7'3"H

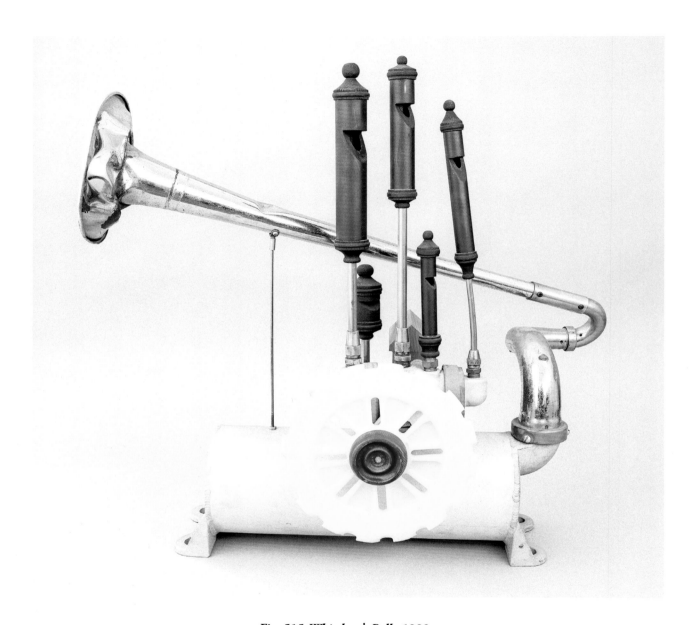

Fig. 515 *Whistles & Bells,* **1983**
Mixed media, 23.5"W x 9.5"D x 20.5"H
Forrester Family Collection

Opposite page:
Fig. 514 *Zappo L'Art Trompeur,* **1983**
Mixed media, 22"H

"Some artists find a particular trope that works for them, and they exhaust that trope. Chuck Forrester had a more expansive, restless approach to making work. I see architectural studies, portraitures, abstractions, assemblage, postmodernism."

—GUY JORDAN, Associate Professor of Art History

The
SERIES
by Joe Nolan

THE SERIES section of the book represents definitive lines of art created mostly during Forrester's sabbaticals from teaching. He used the self-imposed solitude caused by living in a foreign country without native language fluency to his advantage by immersing himself in his own thoughts to produce wildly creative ideas. From the mystical *Aspects of a Portrait* to the clever *Double Image* to the lofty floating sails of *Windjammer,* you are in for a treat.

Aspects of a Portrait

THIS SERIES WAS CREATED during Forrester's sabbatical from Austria to England and then Spain in 1971 and 1972. The sculptures were cast in the Ramon Villa Art Foundry in Valls, Spain.

With this series, Forrester applied his signature hand for figurative sculpture before disassembling the viewer's expectations of the form. Masterful, but playful—this series finds Forrester making seriously sly.

Eucharist (fig. 389, 1971) is one of the most compelling pieces in this series. A low, wide, heavy bronze vase sprouts the shape of a shrouded head decorated with a bunch of grapes. Like Forrester's portraits of the authors of the Gospels, *Eucharist* leans into abstraction in an effort to embody the mystery of the central sacrament of Christianity. The shroud over the face of the Christ figure recalls both the Shroud of Turin and the extra-biblical story of Saint Veronica who comforted Jesus by offering him her handkerchief to wipe his face while he carried his cross to his execution. According to early church history, Jesus's face miraculously appeared on Veronica's handkerchief, but Forrester doesn't reveal his visage.

Lady with Goldilocks (fig. 382, 1971) offers another hidden portrait. This small bronze sculpture is one of Forrester's most gorgeous abstract works, featuring a snug series of columns which curve into a dramatic wave-like arch. It's a beautiful work to behold from any angle, but discerning viewers might be able to spot the profile of a woman's face if they look at the piece just right.

Fruithead (fig. 383, 1971) and *Wind-blown Scarf* (fig. 387, 1971) are both more blatantly humorous works that still manage to play with viewers' expectations of what a portrait bust can be. And *Temporal Sensors* (fig. 401.1, 1972) goes one step further, spotlighting the sensory elements of the head—eyes, ears, nose, and mouth—in a cubist deconstruction of the fundamental elements of portraiture. This work is emblematic of this series as a whole, and its subversive take on the genre of portrait sculpture is as insightful as it is unsettling.

Fig. 389 *Eucharist*, 1971
Bronze, 15.5"W x 8"D x 19"H
Forrester Family Collection

Fig. 382 *Lady with Goldilocks,* 1971
Bronze, 11.5"W x 9"D x 18"H
Forrester Family Collection

Alternate view of *Lady with Goldilocks*

Fig. 383 *Fruithead,* **1971**
Bronze, 6.5"W x 11"D x 18"H
Forrester Family Collection

Fig. 387 *Wind-blown Scarf,* 1971
Bronze, 19"H
Western Kentucky University

Fig. 401.1 *Temporal Sensors,* 1972
Bronze, 7"H
Forrester Family Collection

Opposite page:
Fig. 378 *Portrait with Garlands,* 1971
Bronze, 18"W x 9"D x 17"H
Forrester Family Collection

Double Image

FORRESTER'S DOUBLE IMAGE SERIES explores repetition, reflecting forms and the play between positive and negative space. These works were created while Forrester was on sabbatical in Prague, Czechoslovakia, in 1985. This series is typically diverse and finds Forrester making use of a wide variety of materials and techniques, taking everything from carpentry tools, Bible stories, fruit, and even Barbie dolls as his subjects.

Figure Head (fig. 523, 1983) features repeating elements, which is a common theme throughout this series. In this work Forrester shows us the reiterating ribs of a skeletal sailing vessel—the work is displayed on a gorgeous oval slab of blue-green marble that evokes a deep and dark sea. Forrester replaced the traditional carved figurehead decoration of a woman with the form of a Barbie doll, complete with separated joints typical of the plastic dolls and the smoothed-over pubic region which seems particularly weird and eerie in this context.

Pears—Mother and Child (fig. 420.1, 1978) continues the repetition theme and lets Forrester indulge his love of puns by offering viewers a "pair" of "pears." The pears' reflective surfaces allowed Forrester to double-down on his repeating images theme.

Two-Headed Hammer (fig. 542, 1986) is exactly what the title claims: a reworking of a pair of regular wooden-handled hammers into a somewhat monstrous hybrid. It's one of Forrester's simplest works, but it's striking—no pun intended—nonetheless.

On the opposite end of the spectrum, Forrester's sculpture *Lot's Wife Returns* (fig. 531, 1985) is one of his most conceptually sophisticated: The biblical character was turned into a pillar of salt for disobeying God. Here, Forrester created a kind of sculptural-slow-motion effect, picturing Lot's wife walking out of her sodium prison as a series of separate figures that read like the sequential drawings that make up an animated sequence. At the time, it was a controversial piece, and one Nashville college was reluctant to show it. It's an inspired interpretation that Forrester pulled off with an assured hand.

Fig. 523 *Figure Head,* 1983
Aluminum, 27.5"W x 4"D x 15"H
Forrester Family Collection

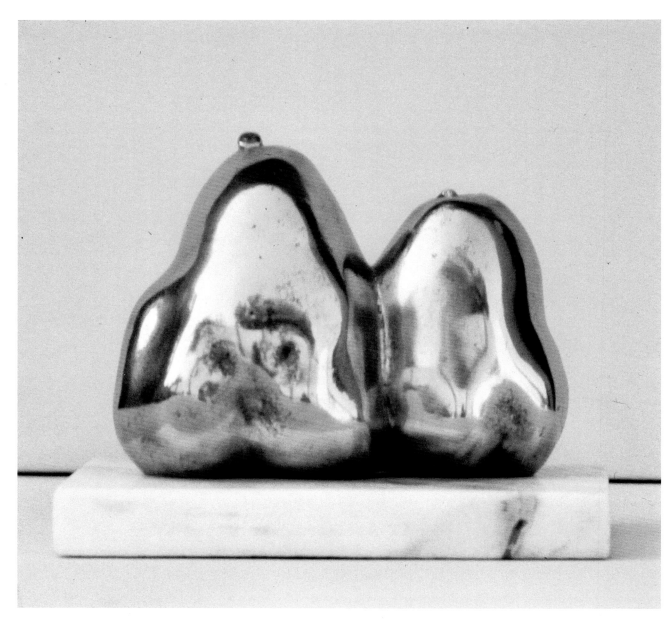

Fig. 420.1 *Pears–Mother and Child,* 1978
Bronze, 4.5"H
Western Kentucky University

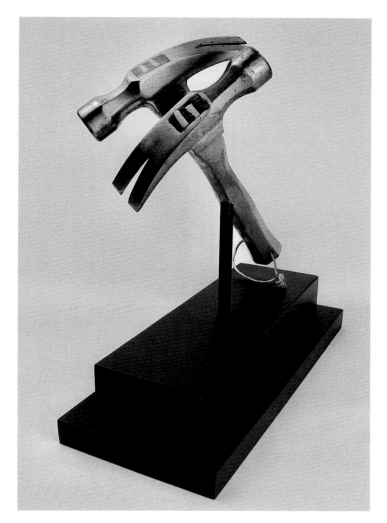

Fig. 542 *Two-Headed Hammer,* 1986
Wood, steel & leather, 13.5"W x 6"D x 13"H
Forrester Family Collection

Below:
Alternate view of *Two-Headed Hammer*

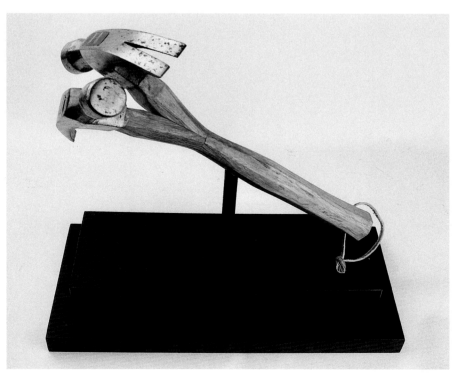

Fig. 526 *Trail Blazer,* 1984
Aluminum, 45.25"H x 8.5" diameter
Forrester Family Collection

Opposite page:
Fig. 531 *Lot's Wife Returns,* 1985
Bronze, 11"H
Carol Winter, Philadelphia, PA

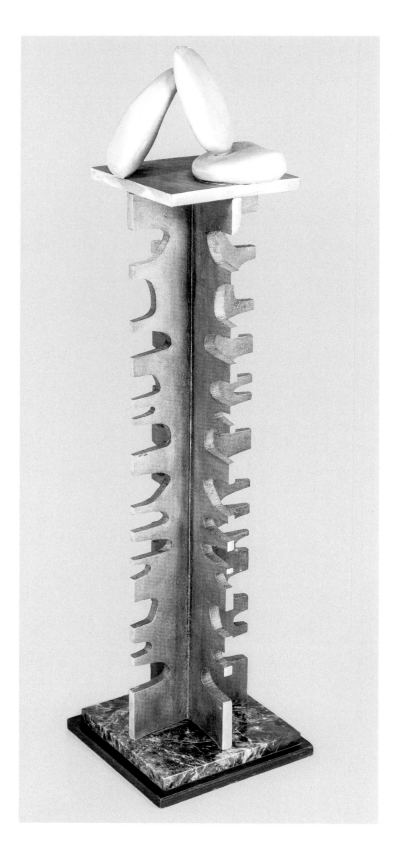

Phantasy

THIS SERIES OF FANTASTICAL FORMS is as magical as it is muscular. Forrester deployed his talent for detailed realism in these works, seducing viewers into surreal scenes and narratives.

Forrester finished *Peace Sign* (fig. 358, 1970) in the middle of the Vietnam War era, six years after the Gulf of Tonkin resolution and five years before the fall of Saigon. This work features a right hand forming the titular greeting with its two raised fingers. Instead of attaching the hand to a forearm, Forrester gave it a pair of legs with their feet pointing in the opposite direction, away from the viewer. This arrangement makes the plump parts of the palm resemble the buttocks of a walking figure. An alternate name Forrester considered was "Mash Symbol," a nod to the logo for Robert Altman's 1970 film *M*A*S*H* which featured a similar walking hand design, but with distinctly feminine legs and feet in high-heeled shoes. The movie version also featured an army helmet perched on top of one of the fingers.

Most of the *Phantasy* series was created over the decade of the 1970s. *Hand Phone* (fig. 361, 1970) and *Hand Ax* (fig. 363, 1970) both play on the theme of combining anatomical hands with the objects mentioned in the titles. A work like *Hand Ax* recalls the kind of old, weird stories associated with ancient myths or *Grimm's Fairy Tales*. But the relative modernity of a work like *Hand Phone* makes it seem more self-consciously surreal.

A hand flat on a marble slab, *Narcissus* (fig. 396, 1972) is one of the most complex pieces in the series. The wrist and forearm rise at an angle before they form the handle of a hand mirror reflecting a face. Forrester made this one even more odd and unsettling by having the long hair of the subject in the mirror's reflection pour out past the edges of the "glass" and wrap around the arm.

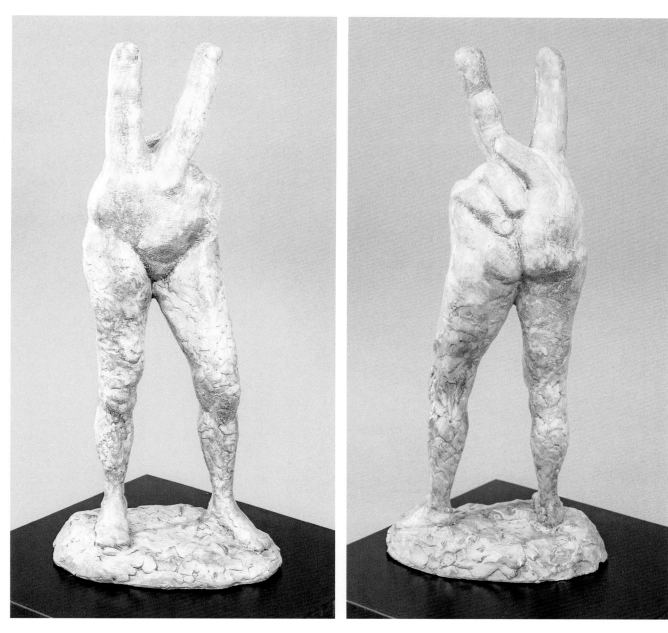

Fig. 358 *Peace Sign* (two views), 1970
Plaster with stain, 7.25"W x 5"D x 17"H
Forrester Family Collection

Fig. 361 *Hand Phone,* 1970
Plaster with stain, 9.75"W x 4"D x 4.75"H
Forrester Family Collection

Fig. 363 *Hand Ax,* 1970
Bronze, 13"W x 3"D x 14"H
Forrester Family Collection

Fig. 364 *Apple's Revenge,* **1971**
Bronze, 5"H
Rabbi Ken Kanter, Chattanooga, TN

Below:
Fig. 566 *Anguish,* **1999**
Plaster with stain, 16.5"W x 7"D x 6.5"H
Forrester Family Collection

Opposite page:
Fig. 396 *Narcissus,* **1972**
Bronze, 7"W x 8"D x 18"H
Forrester Family Collection

Shoe Fantasies

THIS SERIES BASED ON SHOE FORMS includes some of Forrester's most unique works of sculpture along with a number of related drawings and paintings. With *Shoe Fantasies,* he took fashion footwear as a jumping-off point for exploring familiar obsessions: portraiture, architecture, and maritime design.

Works like *Shoe as Portrait* (fig. 467, 1979) and *Kiss My Foot* (fig. 475, 1980) both play at portraiture in their own unique ways. The former features Forrester's familiar high-heeled shoe form—the heel is lifted and it balances on the ball of the sole as if taking a step. The visage of a lovely female face emerges from inside the shoe looking like a lady wearing a scarf over her head. *Kiss My Foot* is more subtle: at first glance it looks like only a sculpture of a high-heeled shoe with a platform sole. But on closer inspection, viewers will notice a sexy pair of lady's lips pursed in a kiss near the toe.

The self-explanatory *Shoe as Architecture* (fig. 470, 1979) isn't really a shoe at all. Here Forrester renders a high ladies' boot in bronze. The boot is unlaced, and it falls open to reveal a classical building featuring a row of stately pillars. The fantastic details and the surreal juxtaposition of the titular elements offer an unlikely, but winning, combination.

Forrester's *Shoe Ship* designs are some of his most recognizable works. *Shoe Ship* (fig. 469, 1979) and *Shoe Ship II* (fig. 487, 1979) both transform his beloved shoe forms into the hulls of sailing ships. With the shoe form upside down, the arch of the shoe becomes the deck, and the long, spiked heel becomes the ship's main mast.

Other works such as *Shoe Box* (fig. 472, 1980) and *Fly Me* (fig. 480, 1981) offer much lighter, less conceptual, and visually sophisticated takes on this series which Forrester created between 1978 and 1979 while on sabbatical and traveling through Italy, Greece, and Yugoslavia.

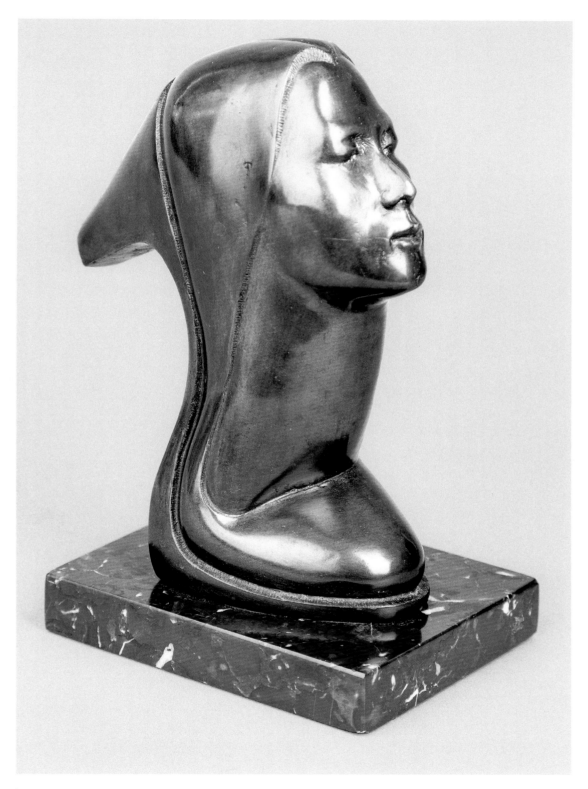

Fig. 467 *Shoe as Portrait,* 1979
Bronze, 3"W x 6.75"D x 9"H
Forrester Family Collection

Shoe Fantasies and Two-Dimensional Works

ARTIST'S STATEMENT BY CHARLES FORRESTER, OCTOBER 1981

THESE SCULPTURES and related drawings were conceived in Rome, Italy, and Athens, Greece, where I lived from late December 1978 until the summer of 1979. The weather was uncharacteristically cold in Rome, and my fingers were too cold to draw in my room or in the unheated cafés. After three weeks, I went to Athens, where I was able to afford a warm room and to begin a record of ideas and impressions in my sketchbook.

I had originally hoped to unite the organic quality of my bronze sculptures with the materials and techniques of my sculptures with wires and tubes. In the beginning I recorded ideas and impressions in my sketchbook. Each morning I worked in my room; in the afternoon I went to visit the ancient ruins, museums and churches.

Finally in Athens, I recognized that the classical and foreign flavor of the city was leading me to the traditional materials of clay and plaster. I began to model a sculpture in clay, and the completed sculpture was cast in plaster. Each succeeding sculpture, taken from the ideas in my sketchbook, was also put into clay and then into plaster. The ruins, the architecture, the people in the streets, even the Greek alphabet, were fertile territory for a sculptor recording his reactions to a different society and visual scene.

I returned to Italy in early April via Yugoslavia. In Rome, I settled down to the same routine I had in Athens, and I created more sculptures in plaster. All of my sculptures began to relate to a common theme which caused me to call them the *Shoe Fantasies* series. The image of a shoe, sometimes fleeting and ambiguous, was present in each sculpture. The sculptures assumed titles which expressed their individual form: *Shoe as Architecture* (fig. 470, 1979), *Shoe Ship* (fig. 469, 1979), *Shoe as Portrait* (fig. 467, 1979), *Shoe Box* (fig. 472, 1980), etc.

The drawings in this exhibit were also developed from my sketchbook and are ideas which seemed to belong to two-dimensional works.

Fig. 470 ***Shoe as Architecture,* 1979**
Bronze, 3.5"W x 8"D x 14"H
Forrester Family Collection

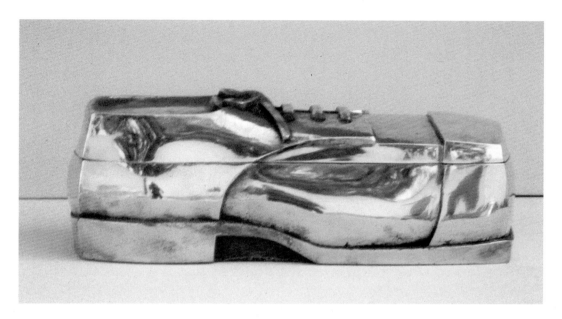

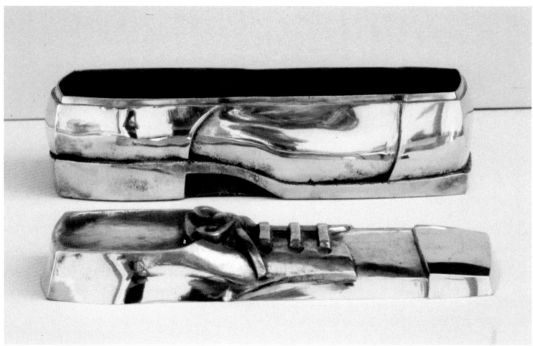

Fig. 472 *Shoe Box* (two views), 1980
Bronze, 14"W
Western Kentucky University

Fig. 469 *Shoe Ship* (two views), 1979
Bronze, 5"W x 9"D x 16"H
Forrester Family Collection

Opposite page:
Fig. 487 *Shoe Ship II,* 1979
Polyester, 7"W x 8"D x 14.75"H
Forrester Family Collection

Fig. 475 *Kiss My Foot,* **1980**
Plaster with paint, 3"W x 7.5"D x 7"H
Forrester Family Collection

Opposite page:
Fig. 480 *Fly Me,* **1981**
Bronze, 4.5"W x 0.5"H x 8.5"D
Forrester Family Collection

Windjammer

FORRESTER'S WINDJAMMER WORKS done in the late 1970s and early 1980s combine elements of architecture and maritime design. Some of these works are feats of engineering, as well as aesthetics.

The *Windjammer* series is one of his only collections of work which are completely bereft of figurative elements. There are no hidden faces here, no hands, no punning nudity. These works embrace things instead of figures, and they also capture space in a way that's more pronounced than in Forrester's other works.

Windjammer I–Sea Frolic (fig. 490, 1981), *Windjammer II–Day Sailer II* (fig. 491, 1981), and *Windjammer III–Day Sailer III* (fig. 492, 1981) all find the artist indulging his obsession with maritime imagery and forms.

Windjammer I–Sea Frolic doesn't offer viewers a ship without a sail as much as a sail without a ship. But instead of sculpting a castaway canvas floating on the sea, the sail of this ghostly, invisible vessel is full of wind and straining toward the horizon.

Likewise, *Windjammer II–Day Sailer II* captures a sail without a ship. In both of these works, the wind is the real star. And there is a quiet confidence at work in Forrester's subtle details, and his manipulation of bonded marble materials makes viewers feel the breeze on their faces and taste the salt on their lips.

Another work in the series is far more architectural, and where the sail forms connect back to Forrester's *Shoe Ships*. A piece like *Windjammer–The Drying Rack* (fig. 485, 1978) has much more in common with his wire suspension works. This collection of collapsible oak panels stretches from a short stack of wooden sticks into a nine-foot-high tower decorated with red plastic panels. The work recalls Japanese structures in its minimal design and raw wooden surfaces, and its collapsibility is another testament to Forrester's knack for intricate structural design.

Fig. 491 *Windjammer II–Day Sailer II,* **1981**
Bonded marble, 8.75"W x 12.75"D x 15.75"H
Forrester Family Collection

FORRESTER TOOK GREAT CARE with the naming of his sculptures. He would record multiple choices for his titles in his records, and mull them over for long periods of time until he was fully satisfied. He often used historical and religious references, and was the master of puns and double entendre. His word play was a source of delight for his followers. In the words of one admirer, "I can't wait to learn the title of this work!" The title often offers the viewer a greater understanding of its creative origin and insight into his intentions for the artwork.

Fig. 485 *Windjammer – The Drying Rack*, **1978**
Oak & plastic, 10"W x 20"D x 105"H
Forrester Family Collection

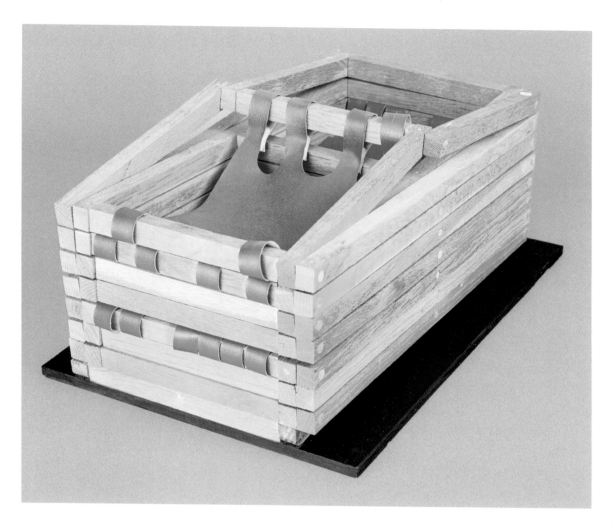

Windjammer – The Drying Rack (collapsed)

Fig. 490 *Windjammer I–Sea Frolic* (two views), 1981
Bonded marble, 10.5"W x 11"D x 11"H
Forrester Family Collection

Fig. 492 *Windjammer III–Day Sailer III*, 1981
Bonded marble, 8"W x 10"D x 19.5"H
Forrester Family Collection

CURRICULUM VITAE

Charles H. Forrester

EDUCATION

1958   BFA, University of Washington

1960   MFA, University of Oregon. Thesis: *An Interpretation of the Four Evangelists in Sculpture*

PROFESSIONAL EXPERIENCE

1958-60   Teaching Assistantship, School of Architecture and Allied Arts, University of Oregon

1963-65   Instructor in Sculpture, Salford Technical College, Salford, England

1965-92   Professor of Sculpture, Western Kentucky University

1966-70   Vice-President and board member, Southern Association of Sculptors

1991   Hosted Fulbright scholar, Jesus Cobo, visiting sculptor from Ecuador

SABBATICALS and RESIDENCIES

1960   Ashland, Oregon, studio

1962   Florence, Italy, studio

1966   Quebec, Canada

1971-72   Vienna, Austria; Brighton, England; and Barcelona, Spain

1978-79   Rome, Italy; Athens, Greece; and Belgrade, Yugoslavia

1982   Cuernavaca, Mexico

1985   Prague, Czechoslovakia

1992   Budapest, Hungary

1995   Istanbul, Turkey

AWARDS and HONORS

1957   Art Students Scholarship Fund Award, University of Washington

1958   Helen Nielsen Rhodes Scholarship, University of Washington

1958   Ruth Nettleton Sculpture Award, University of Washington

1960   First place prize for sculpture, Southern Oregon Art Exhibit

1965   Second place award, Southern Association of Sculptors Regional Show

1966   Award winner, The Parthenon, Nashville, TN

1966   Merit Award, Mid-States Art Exhibition, Evansville Museum of Art, Evansville, IN

1968   Finalist, Lyndon State College Sculpture Commission

1969   Runner-up, University of South Carolina Humanities Sculpture Competition

1974   WKU Summer Fellowship awarded for creative work in sculpture

1977   WKU Faculty Research Grant for the development of tubular sculptures

1980   Merit Award, Owensboro Art Guild–15th Annual Show, Owensboro, KY

1981   Citizens National Bank Purchase Award, Capitol Arts Center, Bowling Green, KY

1988   Second place sculpture prize, Fine Art '88, Capitol Arts Center Gallery, Bowling Green, KY

1989   Best of Show Award, Fine Art '89, Capitol Arts Center Gallery, Bowling Green, KY

BIBLIOGRAPHY

BOOKS & BROCHURES

"Some Younger Northwest Sculptors." *Northwest Review* IV, 2 (Spring 1961), University of Oregon.

Architectural Craftsmen of the Northwest: Illustrated Directory, Seattle, WA. American Craftsmen's Council, 1961.

Harold, Margaret (editor). *Prize-Winning Sculptures,* Book 7, Fort Lauderdale, FL, Allied Publications, Inc., 1967.

Springfield Arts Commission. "Springfield, Oregon Public Art." April 2015. http://www.springfieldartscommission.org/April2015PublicArtBrochureSAC.pdf

ARTICLES

"The Hybrids." *Eugene Register Guard* (Eugene, OR), April 5, 1959.

"For Medford Parks." *Medford Mail Tribune* (Medford, OR), May 12, 1960.

"Sand Pool." *Medford Mail Tribune* (Medford, OR), September 16, 1960.

"Plans Under Way to Complete Work at Jackson Park." *Medford Mail Tribune* (Medford, OR), March 6, 1963.

"Seven little maids—all in a row." *Manchester Evening News* (England), March 11, 1964.

Landsdell, Sarah. "Langston Entry Wins Sculpture '68 Prize: Glass Fiber Used." *Courier-Journal* (Louisville, KY), July 28, 1968.

"Statue will honor late hospital administrator." *Bowling Green Daily News* (Bowling Green, KY), November 26, 1975.

Ward, Lesa. "*Blue Sphere* whirls, floats, quivers with inner energy." *College Heights Herald* (Bowling Green, KY), June 29, 1977.

Beaty, Lisa. "European shoes 'inspire' sculpture." *College Heights Herald* (Bowling Green, KY), September 27, 1979.

McCord, Tom. "Bust-ed." *College Heights Herald* (Bowling Green, KY), March 6, 1980.

McIntosh, Teresa. "Tinker toy: Vandals keep teacher improving sculpture." *College Heights Herald* (Bowling Green, KY), September 24, 1981.

Hieronymus, Clara. "Wood, Metal, Marble, Limestone Works Meld in Sculpture Exhibit." *The Tennessean* (Nashville, TN), July 14, 1985.

"Leu Gallery show opens." *The Tennessean* (Nashville, TN), January 17, 1988.

Jaggers, Ronnie. "Spotlighted Artist: Charles Forrester." *The Amplifier* (Bowling Green, KY), March 4, 2008, print. www.Bgamplifier.com, accessed March 22, 2020, website.

Jones, Rachel Elizabeth. "Mysterious Sculptures Found in Waitsfield Woods." *Vermont's Independent Voice: Seven Day*s, March 16, 2016, print. www.Sevendaysvt.com, accessed March 22, 2020, website.

EXHIBITIONS

ONE-PERSON EXHIBITIONS

1960   University of Oregon Art Museum, Eugene, OR

1961   Rogue Gallery, Medford, OR

1980   Sweetbriar College, Sweetbriar, VA

1980   *Shoe Fantasies,* Ivan Wilson Gallery, Bowling Green, KY

1981   *Shoe Fantasies / Sculpture & Works on Paper,* Ervin G. Houchens Gallery, Bowling Green, KY

1987   Ivan Wilson Gallery, Bowling Green, KY

1988   *Double Image as Sculpture, Sabbatical Show,* Ivan Wilson Gallery, Bowling Green, KY

GROUP EXHIBITIONS

1956-57 Henry Gallery, University of Washington, Seattle, WA

1958   Northwest Sculptor Institute, Portland Art Museum, Portland, OR

1958   University of Oregon Museum of Art, Eugene, OR

1958   *Sculpture Portraits,* Frye Art Museum, Seattle, WA

1959   Vancouver Art Museum, Vancouver, BC

1959   Northwest Sculpture Institute, Vancouver, BC

1959   *The Hybrids Show,* 12th Street Gallery, Eugene, OR

1960   Southern Oregon Art Exhibit, August

1960   Oregon State Fair, Salem, OR

1961   Southern Oregon College, Ashland, OR

1962   *Poor Losers' Show,* Rogue Gallery, Medford, OR

1965   *Southern Association of Sculptors Regional Show,* traveling exhibition

1966   The Parthenon, Nashville, TN

1967-68 *Art in the Embassies* program, US State Department

1967   *Ten Southern Sculptors,* Florida State University, Tallahassee, FL

1967   *Fine Art Festival,* Invitational, Alice Lloyd College, Pippa Passes, KY

1967   *22nd Southeastern Annual Exhibition,* High Museum, Atlanta, GA

1967   Eastern Kentucky University, Richmond, KY

1968   The J.B. Speed Memorial Museum, Louisville, KY

1968   *Southeastern College Art Conference,* University of South Carolina, Columbia, SC

1968   Lyndon State College Sculpture Commission, Lyndonville, VT

1968   High Museum, Atlanta, GA

1968   *Southern Sculpture '68,* traveling exhibition, Southern Association of Sculptors Regional Show

1969   *Carolina Humanities Sculpture Competition,* The University of the South, Sewannee, TN

1969   *Smithsonian Traveling Exhibit,* Washington, D.C.

(Group Exhibitions, continued)

1976 *All-Kentucky Sculpture Show,* Georgetown College Gallery, Georgetown, KY

1976 *Saenger National Jewelry and Small Sculpture Exhibit,* Hattiesburg, MS

1980 *Kentucky Art 1980: Painting, Sculpture, Drawing,* Juried exhibition.
      University of Kentucky Art Museum, Frankfort, KY

1980 Arrowmont School of Arts & Crafts, Gatlinburg, TN

1983 The J.B. Speed Memorial Museum, Café Musee, Louisville, KY

1984 Vanderbilt Hospital show, Nashville, TN

1984 Katzman / Werthan Gallery, Nashville, TN

1985 *Exhibit for Visually Impaired,* Capitol Arts Center, Bowling Green, KY

1985 *Regional Sculptors Exhibition,* Vanderbilt University Club, Nashville, TN

1987 *Regional Sculptors,* Montgomery Bell Academy, Nashville, TN

1987 *Summer Lights Festival,* Ambiance Gallery, Nashville, TN

1988 *Exchange '88-Faculty of WKU,* Krannert Gallery, University of Evansville, IN

1988 *The Nude, Sculpture Inside & Out,* Lexington Art League, Lexington, KY

1989 *Regional Sculptors,* Leu Gallery, Belmont College, Nashville, TN

1993 Chamber of Commerce Art Gallery, Bowling Green, KY

GROUP EXHIBITIONS HELD MULTIPLE TIMES

- *Central South Exhibition,* Nashville, TN (1966, 1967, 1992)
- *Mid-States Art Exhibition,* Evansville Museum of Art, Evansville, IN
  (1966, 1967, 1976, 1980, 1981, 1987, 1988, 1989, 1992)
- *Eight-State Annual Sculpture Exhibition,* The J. B. Speed Memorial Museum, Louisville, KY
  (1975, 1979, 1983, 1984)
- *Annual Drawing & Small Sculpture Exhibition,* Ball State University, Muncie, IN
  (1980, 1981, 1983)
- *Annual Show,* Owensboro Art Guild, Owensboro, KY (1980, 1981, 1987)
- *Annual National Show,* Del Mar College, Corpus Christi, TX (1981, 1982)
- *Annual Juried Art Exhibit,* Capital Arts Center, Bowling Green, KY
  (1981, 1982, 1983, 1987, 1988, 1989, 1990, 1992)
- *WKU Faculty Show,* Ivan Wilson Gallery, Bowling Green, KY
  (1973, 1982, 1987, 1987, 1990, 1991)
- Leu Gallery, Belmont College, Nashville, TN (1986, 1988)
- *Water Tower Annual Regional Exhibit,* Louisville, KY (1987, 1989)
- *Montgomery Bell Annual Sculpture Exhibition,* Nashville, TN (1988, 1989, 1990)
- *Fine Arts '88,* Capitol Arts Center Gallery, Bowling Green, KY (1988, 1989)
- *Jewish Community Center Exhibition,* Nashville, TN (1992, 1994)
- *For the Birds Show,* Centennial Arts Center, Nashville, TN (1990, 1991, 1992)

COMMISSIONS

1959 *The Equestrian,* concrete sculpture, Junior Chamber of Commerce in honor of Oregon's Centennial, Springfield, OR

1960 Outdoor concrete play sculpture, Medford, OR

1961 Outdoor wood playground for Hawthorn Park, Medford Parks & Recreation Department, Medford, OR

1961 *Malvolio, Shylock and King Lear,* life-size busts for the Shakespeare Memorial Theater, Ashland, OR

1961 *Basketball Players,* concrete outdoor sculpture, Bud Wimberly, Texas & Pacific Railroad Yards, Medford, OR

1961 *Evangelist—St. John,* concrete and metal outdoor sculpture, Bundy Art Gallery, Waitsfield, VT

1962 Concrete and metal outdoor sculptures, Red Cross building, Medford, OR

1962 Outdoor wall murals for Mark Goldy, Medford, OR

1963 Outdoor concrete play sculpture for James Park, Glenwood, OR

1964 *Seven Maidens,* cast stone sculpture, Broughton School High School, England

1967 *Two Figures,* bronze sculpture, J.P. Mathews Co, Little Rock, AR

1973 *Ivan Wilson,* bronze portrait life-size bust, Western Kentucky University, Bowling Green, KY

1974 Two sculptures in cast aluminum and corten steel, for outside entrance and interior, Production Credit Association (PCA) building, Glasgow, KY

1975 *Family,* cast stone, Bowling Green-Warren County Hospital, Bowling Green, KY

1983 *Donald Zacharias,* portrait bust, plaster, former president, Western Kentucky University, Bowling Green, KY

1983 *Dr. Dero Downing,* portrait bust, plaster, former president, Western Kentucky University, Bowling Green, KY

1985 *Dr. Kelly Thompson,* portrait bust, plaster, former president, Western Kentucky University, Bowling Green, KY

1985 *Martha II,* laminated wood sculpture, Northern Telecom, Nashville, TN

1986 Two bronze portrait busts for a private patron

1989 *Martha IV,* laminated wood sculpture, Eskind Family Collection, Nashville, TN

1989 *Dr. Kern Alexander,* portrait bust, plaster, former president, Western Kentucky University, Bowling Green, KY

1990 *Dr. John Minton,* portrait bust, plaster, former president, Western Kentucky University, Bowling Green, KY

1992 *Sophia / City Lady,* laminated wood sculpture, Eskind Family Collection, Nashville, TN

1994 *Team Spirit,* cast aluminum, Nelson Metals Products Corp, Glasgow, KY

1996 *Together to the Top,* Bronze sculpture, Lilly Industries, Inc., Bowling Green, KY

Forrester showing a model of his commission, Fig. 138 *The Equestrian.*

WORKS OF ART DIRECTORY

I find his body of work neither interesting, or any of the items desireable to own and have on display or represent of any philosophy or way I might be interpreting the world or merely the area I occupy at any given moment.

Even with his shape/forms which have no obvious similarity to anything of our life or its accessories, dissertations, or core beliefs.